RICHER THAN SPICES

Interior of a Chinese shop filled with commercially exportable remnants of Catherine of Braganza's dowry, which by the early 19th century flooded the American market. Early 19th century, tempera on wood.

GERTRUDE Z. THOMAS

Richer than Spices

How a Royal Bride's Dowry Introduced Cane, Lacquer, Cottons, Tea, and Porcelain to England, and So Revolutionized Taste, Manners, Craftsmanship, and History in both England and America

New York: Alfred · A · Knopf 1965

THIS IS A BORZOI BOOK,
PUBLISHED BY ALFRED A. KNOPF, INC.

FIRST EDITION

Portions of Chapters Five and Six have appeared in slightly different form in Antiques *magazine under the titles "Cane, a Tropical Transplant" in the January 1961 issue and "Lacquer: Chinese, Indian, 'right' Japan, and American" in the June 1961 issue.*

The twenty-nine lines quoted on pages 69–70 are from "Prince Butler's Tale, 1699" as it appears in Dutch and Flemish Furniture *by Esther Singleton, published by McClure, New York, in 1902.*

The two lines by James Cawthorne quoted on page 143 are from A Cycle of Cathay *by William W. Appleton, published by Columbia University Press, New York, in 1951.*

The eight lines quoted on page 198 are from "A lady's Adieu to her Tea-Table" by Philip Fithian as quoted in Life in America *by Marshall Davidson, published by Houghton Mifflin Company, Boston, in 1951.*

Preface

"There is occasions and causes why and wherefore in all things . . ."　　*Henry V, V.i.4.*—SHAKESPEARE

Everything your eye touches within the four walls of your home, has a fascinating story to tell. There is love and intrigue, history and geography, trial, error, and success in each kind of material, in every color, shape, and fragrance. Everything suggests romance as varied as a kaleidoscope, and is every bit as colorful, when all the bits and pieces fall into their proper places.

The homes our earliest colonists left behind them in Europe had changed but little since the Middle Ages. Strong, square shapes of chest and bed were only partly softened by covers of home-dyed woolens. There were touches of rugged grace and of bold color, and there was solid comfort. Little else was known. Little else was dreamed of— except by those few who for love of money or adventure had pushed beyond existing boundaries and had returned with tales and tokens of another world.

It was these tales that teased adventuring merchants, intrepid explorers, and foolhardy navigators to see for themselves and to claim for their sovereigns lands beyond the known horizon. It was tales of Prester John, of Cathay and Cipangu, and hints of the Northwest Passage to the East that kept fresh for centuries the urge for exploration, and the lure of untold wealth in gold and goods.

But it was the tokens—a length of silk, a lacquer chest, some fragrant tea or pungent spices, a porcelain cup or a chattering monkey—that changed the pattern of Renaissance living. And it was the demanding desire for such exotic extravagances that in great measure shaped geography and wrote the history of the world.

Yet more important to you and to me was the way these eastern imports affected our western heritage. Their color lightened the tone of decorations; their shapes inspired every sort of European craftsman; and strange tastes, new smells challenged cooks and tempted gourmets. The whole western world responded to the insinuating influence of the seductive arts of the unknown East.

When in 1662, the Portuguese Princess, Catherine of Braganza, became the bride of England's Charles II, eastern shapes and smells and colors were carried to England by the terms of her dowry. No one dreamed though, at that time, that the reams of words in their marriage contract contained the germs of the Industrial Revolution that fed on India's cotton goods.

Neither could Englishmen guess that the new customs and conventions inherent in Chinese tea and porcelain, when grafted to existing patterns of western living, would evolve into the graceful, sophisticated society of the eighteenth century. Nor did anyone then suspect that one day that same tea would spark the accumulated grievances of unborn American colonists into a severing revolution.

Such were the unrecognized riches that lay hidden in the dowry of Catherine of Braganza. These were the unpredictable ingredients that shaped the core of our own widely varied inheritance.

Acknowledgments

Richer than Spices got its start long years ago when I first began to research the background of American antiques. Its theme—the far-reaching influence of the fabulous dowry of Catherine of Braganza—was formulated during the semester Mr. Edward A. Walton taught me "History of Furniture" at the old Philadelphia Museum School of Design. His imaginative presentation put life into inanimate objects and suggested my story, for which I shall be forever grateful to him.

My research was further stimulated and unwittingly guided by many eminent speakers, especially those of the "Antiques Forums" at Williamsburg, Virginia, and of the "Seminars on American Culture" at Cooperstown, New York, to each of whom I owe a deep debt of gratitude.

Further, I wish to thank the numerous librarians and others who patiently helped me in my search through uncounted volumes in their colleges, institutions, and museums—in England, in Portugal, and, of course, in the United States, especially at Colonial Williamsburg and The Henry Francis duPont Winterthur Museum, Winterthur, Delaware.

I also wish to thank the many museums, libraries, and individuals, on both sides of the world, who so generously either supplied pictures of their treasures or permitted them to be photographed, and then gave me permission to use them as illustrations in this book. The credits for them are given in the list of illustrations.

In particular, I wish to thank Miss Virginia Daiker of the Library of Congress; Miss Ellen Shaffer, Miss Dorothy Litchfield, and Miss Maude Hawthorne of the Free Library of Philadelphia; Miss Marjorie Lyons, librarian, and Mr. Kneeland McNulty, curator of prints at the Philadelphia Museum of Art; Mrs. Dorothy Moorhouse, formerly head librarian of the Ludington Public Library of Bryn Mawr, Pennsylvania; and at the Winterthur Museum, Dr. E. McClung Fleming, Dean of Education, Mr. Milo M. Naeve, Registrar, and Mr. Charles F. Hummel, assistant curator, among others.

In the final analysis, however, *Richer than Spices* owes its very existence in printed form to the continued encouragement of a patient family and interested friends, particularly Mrs. I. O'Conor Pepper, Mrs. John H. Mensel, Mr. S. B. Richards Taylor, Dr. E. McClung Fleming, and Miss Alice Winchester, editor of *Antiques*—each of whom in turn read the manuscript, offered suggestions, and helped it on its way.

To all of these, and to countless anonymous helpers, I dedicate this book with my most heartfelt thanks.

GERTRUDE Z. THOMAS

"Walnut Hill," Villa Nova, Pennsylvania

Contents

Illustrations

RICHER THAN SPICES

The Dowry

"Dowry—That which a wife bringeth her husband in marriage."
— SAMUEL JOHNSON

FROM the seclusion of her cabin, the Infanta of Portugal listened to music made for her entertainment, and dreamed the dreams of a young girl on the way to her wedding. Since her childhood, Catherine of Braganza had hoped someday to marry Charles Stuart. Now that he was King of England, she could hardly believe that her sheltered girlhood was behind her, that at last she was sailing into her future as his Queen.

It was not love, nor was it beauty that had placed her in this position. It was politics, and it was money. Catherine's mother had baited the matrimonial hook well with a dowry of £500,000 in promised cash, free trading rights for English ships in Brazil and the Portuguese East Indies, with also Tangiers and Bombay to be ceded to England.

Tangiers and Bombay, however, were but indistinct specks on an Englishman's map. Free trading rights in Brazil and the East Indies held vague future promise to harassed English shipping. But it was the immediacy of the cash in her dowry—the promised half-million English pounds—that tipped the matrimonial scales in Catherine's favor.

When in 1660 Charles II came to the throne of England, eleven years of Cromwell's puritanical Commonwealth had left a devastated, cheerless land. Everything tainted with royal pretensions had disappeared for political reasons, and religious fanaticism had discouraged or destroyed all that savored of luxury or of personal indulgence. Palaces and castles stood cold and naked, stripped of their elegance and beauty. The churches spared destruction were but skeletons of their former grandeur. The treasury existed in name alone—all wealth had fled the country. This was the England to which Charles returned, with neither private means nor public funds at his command.

From Breda in Holland, where he had kept the semblance of a court-in-exile, Charles traveled to The Hague to receive, in ill-disguised poverty, the delegation of Englishmen that had come to take him home. Samuel Pepys* was shocked to find "in what a sad, poor condition for clothes and money the King was, and all his attendants, . . . their clothes not being worth forty shillings the best of them." According to Pepys, the new King of England was "so joyful" at sight of the ready cash they had brought him "that he called the Princess Royal and Duke of York to look upon it, as it lay in the portmanteau before it was taken out."[1]† Never had Charles seen so much money. For years, only the promise of seldom paid pensions had held his body and soul together.

His was a gallant soul, a handsome body; and ever since his teens he had wandered penniless with his mother from one European court to another. First as Prince of Wales, then as uncrowned King of England, Charles Stuart was considered a poor matrimonial risk from every angle except that of personal attractiveness. He had no money, no kingdom, and no prospects of acquiring either. "La Grande Mademoiselle," first cousin of Louis XIV, would have none of him, neither would the Royal Princess of Orange. As to the various German princesses, he brushed them off with "Oddsfish! They are all dull and foggy!"[2]

With Charles actually seated on the throne of England, political arrangers and royal matchmakers carefully surveyed the narrow circle of

* Samuel Pepys (1633–1703) kept a diary in cipher from 1660 to 1669. He was clerk of the acts of the Navy, secretary to two generals of the fleet, president of The Royal Society in 1684, and sat for many years in the House of Commons. His library and collection of prints are preserved in his old college, Magdalene, Cambridge, England.

† The bibliographical references are at the end of the book. See Notes, pages 201 ff.

suitable eligibles for the most advantageous connection. Of those that had spurned him in his leaner days, Charles now would hear nothing. There was one princess, however, whom he had never seen in his shabby wanderings—one who had been carefully duenna-shielded from the intrigues of the world. She was Catherine, daughter of the 8th Duke of Braganza, recently crowned John IV of Portugal. As Infanta of Portugal, Catherine of Braganza had quite the largest dowry in all of Europe.

Charles was of that breed of men to whom a pretty face was all-important. Carefully, he studied the large, soft eyes and the shy face in the miniature sent him for approval. Hopefully, he remarked: "That person cannot be unhandsome."[3] At that point no one bothered to tell him she spoke not a word of English.

Catherine, for her part, had certainly heard about the new King of England. When she was six, her father had tried in vain to arrange a betrothal with Charles, the then eleven-year-old heir apparent. After that plan had failed, the long years of her girlhood marked time but slowly within the tapestry-hung chambers of the Royal Palace in Lisbon, where she was constantly surrounded by disciplinary, protective duennas, with never a man in sight except an occasional relative. "She hath hardly been tenn tymes out of the Palace in her life,"[4] wrote the British consul at Lisbon in 1660, and added, "In five years tyme shee was not out of doores." But over embroidery canvas or painting easel, her mind was free to dream of the man she still hoped some day to marry.

When nuptial negotiations with Charles were again revived, Catherine was just past twenty-one. But little did she care—if indeed she even knew of the arrangements—that it was her fabulous dowry which had tipped the scales of international connivance in her favor. All that the consul could report at the time was that "Shee is as sweete a disposition[ed] Princes as everr was borne, and a lady of excellent partes, and bred hugely retired," but when "she harde [heard] of his Maties intentions to make her Queen of Ingland, . . . shee hath been to visit two saintes in the city; and very shortly shee intends to pay her devotions to some saintes in the country."[5]

Now, a full year later, in the spring of 1662, her tiny bridal fleet was floating down the Tagus to the sea, escorting Catherine aboard that same *Royal Charles* which had carried her prince from Holland to his English throne. Even as she pondered on her future, her most prophetic

1) Catherine of Braganza at twenty-two, as she looked to Charles II when he married her. Her dress with the wide Portuguese farthingale is black, trimmed in silver lace, with slashings and petticoat of pale gray. By or after Dirk Stoop, c. 1660–1.

2) Catherine of Braganza just stepping from the end of the Royal Gallery into the Portuguese bark which ferried her out into the Tagus where the *Royal Charles* of the English fleet waited to carry her to England. One of a set of seven engravings by Dirk Stoop, 1662.

thoughts could never have foreseen the exciting changes the assorted cultures of her dowry would bring to England. One in her retinue, though, sensed the world-shaking consequences and in figurative verse spelled them out for posterity. Speaking of Catherine, he wrote:

> *The Royal* Charles, *in her ha's shipt in more.*
> *Than all the* Lisbon *Caracks* did before.*
> *Both* Indies *in a trice, where ere she comes,*
> *She out-ballances all Wealth, Perfumes, and Gummes.*
> Tagus *does flow to Thames, and now* White-hall
> *H'as found Capacity for Portugall.*
> London *ha's swallow'd* Lisbon, *Englands Coast*
> *Hath gain'd more from us, then [sic] our Conquests boast . . .*[6]

For Catherine was a product of Portugal—the crossroads of the world— to whose shores generations of exploring traders had carried the luxuries of the East. Because of Catherine, the results of their daring would be gathered and refined by generations of Englishmen, then scattered again at a profit throughout the expanding world.

* A carrack was a Portuguese square-rigged, shallow-draft three-master of 200 tons, used as both merchantman and warship in the fifteenth and sixteenth centuries.

Catherine's countrymen were well entitled to the first fruits of exploration, for they had methodically, and as scientifically as the times allowed, charted their courses to prove actual the alluring legends circulated about lands and men. Even before the Mohammedan Turks captured Constantinople in 1453 and closed it to Christian trade, the Portuguese had searched for a sea route to those lands of which Marco Polo had written a hundred and fifty years before. All through the fifteenth century, and even later, sea pilots, mariners, and seagoing merchants based their navigational calculations on his description of the world as he had found it—eighty-five manuscript copies of which are still preserved in museums and libraries today.

So, as the gates slammed shut on the overland route from the East, Prince Henry of Portugal, together with the best nautical minds of his country, studied Marco Polo's *Book* and those "handy maps" on sailing called *portolani,* and redoubled their efforts to find a water route to

3) A statue of Marco Polo in the garb of a Portuguese sailor of the 16th century. One of four guarding the portal of the compound surrounding *Wat Po,* a temple in Bangkok, Siam, erected by the Portuguese in the 16th century and still standing today.

those centers of trade the caravans had tapped—the incredible places Marco Polo had seen.

For twenty-odd years Marco Polo had zigzagged his way eastward across Asia, supposedly even through the indefinite dominions of Prester John, then had wandered across Cathay* and beyond on missions for the great Kublai Khan, to whose brilliant court he was attached as councilor. On his return to Venice in 1295, Marco Polo told all who would listen of cotton in India that grew six yards tall; of a city in China where all people dressed in silk, yet still had plenty to spare for foreign merchants; and of fortunes to be had in Java in "pepper, nutmegs, spikenard, galangal, cubebs, cloves and all the other valuable spices and drugs."[7] But his tales only earned for him the sobriquet "Marco dei Millioni"—Marco of the Millions—among his neighbors, for they thought he exaggerated a million times. To this day at carnival time in Venice, he is still caricatured by the tattered clowns in their exaggerated gestures, as fantastic as formerly were thought his tales. Yet he had seen it all, and more, with the appraising eyes of a Venetian merchant through whose hands had passed the rich East-West commerce of the Medieval world.

These were the riches Prince Henry of Portugal sought for his country. As the third surviving son of John I of Portugal and of Philippa, daughter of England's John of Gaunt, he was comparatively free to indulge his own pursuits without much concern for royal succession. After distinguishing himself as a soldier, he turned to the sea and exploring, which earned him the byname of "the Navigator." For the rest of his life he lived with dedication at the naval arsenal at Sagres near Cape St. Vincent, from where he could watch the Atlantic Ocean lash the southernmost tip of Portugal and planned and charted ways of how to reach the lands beyond. Within his fortress-castle he gathered about him the best nautical minds of the day—astronomers, navigators,

---

* *Cathay was the early name for that part of east Asia which extends north from the Yangtze River to the Great Wall, and which at times was dominated by the Manchurian Tartars. South China, which continued to cling to its old Sung culture, was called "Mangi." These names stuck well past Marco Polo's time, even though all of China was then under the control of Kublai Khan. In the sixteenth century, when Europeans discovered South China by way of the Spice Islands, they still spoke of Cathay as beyond to the north, only to be reached by a still undeveloped "northwest" or "northeast" passage, depending upon from where.*

cartographers, and eminent Arabic and Jewish mathematicians—who schooled pilots and sea captains in map and instrument making and in the newest methods of navigation.

From there at Sagres, he sent one lateen-rigged caravel* after another sailing south along the west coast of Africa to find the treasures of the East. The first to round the point known as the "Cape of Storms" was helplessly blown there by thirteen consecutive days of savage winds and sea. All that followed and returned brought back rumors of the priest-king Prester John and tales of men turned black by a searing sun. In Prince Henry's lifetime though, none found the sea route to Cathay, nor to Java and the aromatic Isles of Spice, but all now knew the tip of Africa as the "Cape of Good Hope."

Rumors of him who styled himself "Presbyter Joannes, by the power and virtue of God and of the Lord Jesus Christ, Lord of Lords,"[8] had circulated through the western world since the closing years of the twelfth century. The indeterminate boundaries of his powerful empire of seventy-two tribute-paying kingdoms extended, in his own words, "over the three Indies." There are still extant today almost one hundred manuscript copies of Prester John's extraordinary letter introducing himself to the world; eight are in the British Museum.

For centuries, no dignitary of the Renaissance world could well afford not to pay homage to this august personage, when even distantly approaching his sophistical domain. In fact, Christopher Columbus, as emissary of Ferdinand and Isabella, carried with him as he sailed into the setting sun "greetings and increase of good fortune" addressed "To the most serene Prince————,"[9] the blank to be completed with the name of the first worthy encountered, be he Kublai Khan or Prester John.

Kublai Khan, who had added South China to Cathay and had founded the Mongol dynasty, had been dead two hundred years when Columbus discovered America. And according to Marco Polo, Prester John had been personally killed by Kublai's father, Jenghiz Khan, in the twelfth century. Even so, the search for the illusive Prester John and his incredible empire continued to intrigue the imaginations of generations of adventurers.

All through the fifteenth century, ruling princes still addressed them-

* A caravel is a Portuguese 100-ton lateen-rigged vessel of the fourteenth and fifteenth centuries.

selves to "Prester John of the Indies," but some directed their epistles to that Christian potentate now rumored to reside somewhere in Africa, perhaps Abyssinia. So persistent were these reports that King Manoel I of Portugal commissioned Vasco da Gama to search there for Prester John. In 1497, four specially built vessels sailed for Africa and safely rounded the Cape, as Henry the Navigator had believed they could. In port after port up the east coast they looked for the royal will-o'-the-wisp. When they failed to find Prester John, the four little ships struck out across the Indian Ocean into the secret reaches of the Arab trade routes.

In the opinion of Vasco da Gama, any infidel territory was legitimate loot for a believer. In fact, the Pope, Alexander VI, had in 1494 divided the newly-to-be-discovered lands of the world between Portugal and Spain. The line of demarcation was drawn north to south through the Atlantic Ocean, 370 leagues west of the Portuguese Cape Verde Islands —Spain to have claim to all lands found west of the arbitrary line, and Portugal to all lands discovered to the east. So it was that Spain explored both the Americas, except for that part of Brazil that happened to lie east of the specified meridian. And so it was, among other reasons, that Vasco da Gama found himself before Calicut on the west coast of India, which at that time was the threshold to all the inland wealth of Asia.

Vasco da Gama's reception at Calicut was far from cordial. "May the devil take you! What brought you hither?"[10]—or the Arabic equivalent —were reputedly the first words to greet him. For the taking of Calicut by Vasco da Gama was the beginning of the vast eastern empire that made the King of Portugal "Lord of the Conquest, Navigation, and Commerce of India, Ethiopia, Arabia, and Persia," as confirmed by Pope Alexander VI in 1502.

After Calicut, every strategic spot on the western, the Malabar, coast of India was claimed by Portugal with Goa on the Arabian Sea as the seat of administration. Then on the Malay Peninsula the Portuguese established a station at Malacca, and eventually claimed the whole Malay Archipelago for themselves. For one swashbuckling century they bribed, threatened, bargained, fought, and converted without much opposition, until their empire included such strategic spots as Ceylon, Sumatra, and the Spice Islands, now called the Moluccas.

At Canton though, that same approach only delayed their trade with

China. As early as 1517, a Portuguese carrack had tacked its way eighty miles up the Pearl River, between thousands of outlandish trading junks, to the very edge of the busy waterfront spread below the city walls of Canton. Imperiously the Portuguese announced their arrival with a deafening salvo of cannons. No amount of later protestations could convince the indignant Chinese that the salute had been anything less than a threat. After forty years of wrangling and surreptitious trade—even then, ostensibly only as a reward for having cleared plundering pirates out of surrounding waters—the Portuguese were allowed to settle on the little rocky point of Macao that juts out into the Pearl River where it joins the China Sea. Because piracy continued, Chinese junks were forbidden to sail beyond their own coastal waters, and the Portuguese subsequently handled all Chinese foreign shipping with profit to themselves.

As for Japan, it was a storm in 1542 that blew the Portuguese there. After almost a century of trade, Portuguese Jesuit missionaries were accused of meddling in Japanese politics and, in consequence, all Portuguese nationals were summarily evicted from the islands in 1638. Not another Portuguese ship could touch Japan on penalty of being burned with all her cargo, and every human executed. The terminating message, "Think no more of us, just as if we were no longer in the world,"[11] closed forever to Portugal the rich trade of Japan.

In spite of these misadventures, the exotic wealth of the East that was gathered from the widely scattered shores of Asia continued to pour into the ports of Portugal. Instead of trading in Venice or Genoa, the merchants of Europe now traveled to Lisbon for gum-lac, indigo, and myrrh; cinnamon, mace, ginger, pepper, and cloves; for precious gems and "parcels of pearls"; for raw and "wrought" China silks; for cotton goods called baftas, broderas, cashees, dorbellas,* and many more whose names have long since been forgotten.

By 1662, when Catherine of Braganza sailed to her Charles in England, the little kingdom of Portugal was still able to gild its princess with the richest dowry in Europe—despite sixty years of subservience to Spain, the ever-increasing competition of the aggressive Dutch, and

*According to explanations sprinkled throughout A Calendar of The Court Minutes, etc., of the East India Company, the term baftas applied to more than one kind of cotton goods. Broderas were calicoes from Baroda; cashees were a special kind of fine calico or muslin; and dorbellas were calicoes from Tatta.

4) A Portuguese ship with green sails on a green-blue sea painted in watercolor on gold paper. She was being driven by a storm to seek shelter in a Japanese harbor and was flying a Japanese flag at the stern and Portuguese flags amidships. One of a pair of six-fold Japanese paper screens, called *"nambu byobu."* 17th century.

the sporadic trading efforts of the struggling English East India Company.

To Charles, to his impoverished court, and to England, Catherine's dowry was only as rich as the number of money pieces mentioned, for those were "almost double to what any King had ever received in Money by any Marriage."[12] As for the rest of the dowry, it was condemned by ignorance.

Free trading rights for English shipping in the ports of Brazil and the Portuguese East Indies were suspected of being but a grandiose gesture without value. The ceding of Tangiers, African counterpart to Gibraltar, made little impression on an England too poor to maintain it. As for Bombay, included to assure the Portuguese an ally in the East against the openly hostile Dutch, it was contemptuously called a "pestilential swamp" by contemporary English chroniclers—hardly an asset. However, the Portuguese Ambassador at the Court of St. James's had glowingly pictured the "Island of Bombayne" as sprinkled with towns and studded with castles overlooking spacious bays and had contended its possession "would be a vast Improvement to the East-India Trade. And . . . might reasonably be valued above the Portion in Money."[13] Not even in their most exaggerated enthusiasm could the Portuguese perceive how literally true their optimism would prove!

But in the spring of 1662, England was more in need of ready money than of a rosy future. For that pecuniary reason Catherine's departure from Portugal met several delays, while the English were "forced to have some clashing . . . about payment of the portion, before [they] could get it."[14] Even then, there was but little actual cash, for Catherine's mother had borrowed heavily against the dowry to finance Portuguese resistance to Spain. Pushed to fulfill her promise to England, the Queen of Portugal substituted her jewels and plate, filled the holds of the bridal fleet with sugar, and added bills of exchange to round out a doubtful half of Catherine's portion of £500,000. As for the rest, Portugal agreed to pay the "other Moiety within the Space of a Year."[15] Of the little money Catherine did bring with her, Samuel Pepys stored three chests of Portuguese crusadoes overnight in his cellar, and "made the maids to rise and light a candle, and set it in the dining-room, to scare away thieves."[16] Two days later he watched "some thousands of . . . crusadoes weighed, and . . . find that 3,000 comes to about £530 or 40 generally."[17]

5) Charles II, at the age of thirty-nine, seven years after he married Catherine of Braganza. From a mezzotint by William Sherwin, supposedly the earliest by any English artist, and dedicated to Prince Rupert, cousin of Charles, who is credited with introducing the art into England. Dated 1669.

No thought of money, however, crossed the mind of Charles as he rushed to greet Catherine at Portsmouth. It was the man in him, not the King, who noticed first that this wife he had never seen before had a "face . . . not so exact as to be called a beauty, though her eyes are excelent good," nor had she "anything in her face that in the least degree can shoque one." In fact, he wrote his Chancellor, Edward Hyde: "She hath as much agreeableness in her looks altogether as ever I saw, and if I have any skill in visiognimy, which I think I have, she must be as good a woman as ever was borne."[18] Charles II, at that moment, considered himself very fortunate that the personal part of the complicated international marriage barter held for him such pleasant prospects. As ecstatically as any normal bridegroom, he blurted out: "I cannot easily tell you how happy I think myselfe; and I must be the worst man living (which I hope I am not) if I be not a good husband."[19]

Time and circumstances have a way of their own with prophecies, and it didn't take long for Charles to prove himself wrong. And wrong, too, were the political pessimists who could see no good for England in any of the Portuguese concessions of Catherine's dowry. As well for them that they could not, for nothing short of a visionary madman would have been able even to hint at the social changes Catherine's dowry would provoke before many more years were to elapse.

CHAPTER TWO

The East India Company

Deus Indicat—*motto of The Governour and Merchants of London Trading into the East Indies*

DURING the century in which the Portuguese had swept clean the Indian Ocean for themselves, the English vainly probed the American coastline from Labrador to Virginia seeking a Northwest Passage to Cipangu, fabled land of silk and spices that was Japan. The occasional returning carrack they pirated from Spain or Portugal only whetted English appetites for a greater share of the eastern silks, spices, indigo, and copper with which she was loaded.

Since the Crusades, Europe had known limited luxuries from the Orient; but until the sixteenth century, not much more than pepper and spices had trickled as far north as England. Important for food preservation, spices, especially pepper, had determined for centuries the early trade routes of the world. In northern countries such as England, when grasslands turned brown in the fall, animals were slaughtered for food, because there were no facilities to winter them. Meat for the winter table had to be dried, salted, or pickled with quantities of pepper and spices. Later, when it was boiled to the verge of extinction, pepper, nutmeg, and allspice helped make it palatable, or attempted to smother the unhappy results of faulty preservation.

Beyond the sheer necessities of existence, spices also substituted for cleanliness and for ventilation. When aging rushes were reduced to musty matting under many feet, cloves were strewn among them to change the flavor of the atmosphere. Cloves, cinnamon, and allspice were layered with rose petals for a potpourri, or were mashed to a paste, then shaped and dried into little cones that smoldered incense in a stuffy room. Ladies and gentlemen alike carried about with them a nutmeg in a little silver box fitted with a tiny grater, ready to season indifferent food; and a spicy pomander hung around many a throat to ward off both suffocation and illness. Pepper and spices sifted through the whole fiber of Renaissance living, and the trade in these was basic to the economy.

The long-established pattern of European trade with the East changed suddenly in 1453 when Constantinople fell to the Moham-medan Turks. Spices and oriental trade goods could still be had, but now Turks, Moors, and Arabs each demanded tribute on every saddle-bag traveling west. Luxuries could bear a premium, but the need of maintaining an adequate supply of pepper and spices at acceptable prices spurred European merchants and navigators to push their com-petitive search for a sea route to the East.

Even though the Portuguese were the first to find their way around the Cape of Good Hope, they still had to depend upon the Dutch, who had been middlemen for the old overland trade from Asia, to distribute their cargoes through the north of Europe. But in 1594, that arrange-ment ceased. Since 1581, Portugal had been held in fee by Spain. Now in 1594, six years after Spain's "invincible" Armada had been destroyed by the English, Philip II of Spain closed Portugal's port of Lisbon to both English and Dutch trade, for he was also at war with Holland. In reprisal, the Dutch fought their way to the Spice Islands, expelled the Portuguese from Bantam in Java, and clinched for themselves the monopoly of the spice trade. By the end of the century, pepper sold on the London market for eight shillings a pound, double the price of 1580.

In the meantime, English "Merchant Adventurers" had traded through the Baltic into Russia, bargained their way across the Mediter-ranean as far as the Levant, and bartered what they could up and down the west coast of Africa. With the blessing of the first Elizabeth, English "Free Booters" sailed the Atlantic hoping for a chance meeting with a

Spanish treasure galleon; traded and looted in the West Indies; and in 1580, under Sir Francis Drake, sailed home to Plymouth with booty estimated at about four million Spanish dollars, plundered in three years of piracy around the world.

But it was the *Madre de Dios,* a huge carrack, "one of the greatest receit [a vessel of trade] belonging to the crowne of Portugall . . . ," which, when brought into Dartmouth Harbor on the seventh of September 1592, lifted the edge of the eastern horizon for England. The "true report [of the capture] . . . prepared by the honor. Sir Walter Raleigh" has been preserved by Richard Hakluyt, the Elizabethan geographer, in his collection of *Principal Navigations, Voyages, Traffiques & Dis-*

6) A map of the world marked with those trade centers of the 17th century made important through Catherine's dowry and the East India Company, and a few of the early explorers' routes that opened up the East to western trade.

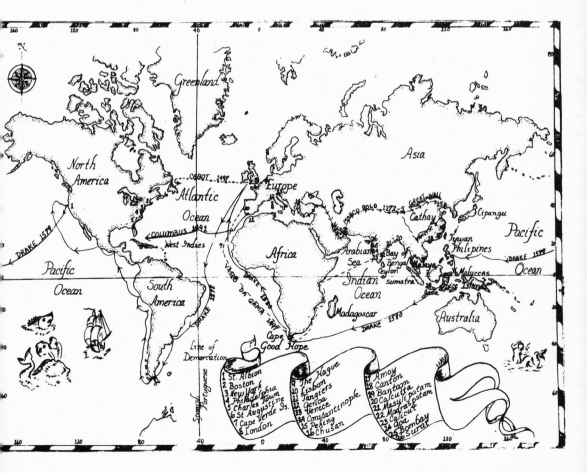

7) Armed cargo vessels used in the East India trade. Headpiece of a poem entitled "How to Get Riches," dated 1736. From George Bickham's *The Universal Penman,* 1743.

coveries of the English Nation. In it Raleigh relates that more than a dozen of Elizabeth's choice captains had lain in wait for thirty-six days that summer to capture the Portuguese fleet of five carracks sailing home from Goa. Six or seven leagues west of Flores, an island in the Azores, were congregated the best ships of England, drawn from the fleets of Sir John Hawkins, Sir Walter Raleigh, and others, including the *Golden Dragon* captained by Christopher Newport, who later was to settle Virginia. ". . . al [sic] these ships . . . spread themselves abroad from the North to the South, ech [sic] ship two leagues at the least distant from another."[1]

In that manner was the proud *Madre de Dios* taken, filled with a wealth that "would arise nothing disanswerable to expectation; but that the variety and grandure of all rich commodities would be more than sufficient to content both the adventurers desire & the souldiers travell." The "poringer of white porselyn, and a cup of greene porselyn," which Lord Burghley had once given Elizabeth as a New Year's gift, were now as nothing to the superabundance of East Indian treasures spread out before the Queen.

The sixteen-hundred-ton carrack, as she lay at anchor in Dartmouth Harbor with her sails furled, "had full 900 of those [tons] stowed with the grosse bulke of marchendise." And Sir Walter Raleigh, "To give you a taste (as it were) of the commodities," enumerated "a generall particularity of them, according to the catalogue taken at Leaden hall" the week after the *Madre de Dios* was brought to port. "Where upon good view it was found, that the principall wares after jewels (which were no doubt of great value, though they never came to light) consisted of spices, drugges, silks, callicos, quilts, carpets and colours &c. The spices were pepper, cloves, maces, nutmegs, cinamom, greene ginger: the drugs were benjamin, frankincense, galingale, mirabolans, aloes zocotrina, camphire: the silks damasks, taffatas, sarcenets, altobassos, that is, counterfeit cloth of gold, unwrought China silke, sleaved silke, white twisted silke, curled cypresse. The calicos were book-calicos, calico launes, broad white calicos, fine starched calicos, course white calicos, browne broad calicos, browne course calicos. There were also canopies, and course diaper-towels, quilts of course sarcenet and of calico, carpets like those of Turkey; whereunto are to be added the pearle, muske, civet and amber-griece."

But that was not all. "The rest of the wares were many in number but lesse in value; as elephants teeth, porcellan vessels of China, coconuts, hides, eben-wood as blacke as jet, [and] bedsteds of the same . . ." According to Raleigh, "All which piles of commodities [were] by men of approved judgement rated . . . to no lesse than 150000 li. sterling, which being divided among the adventurers (whereof her Majesty was the chiefe) was sufficient to yeeld contentment to all parties."[2]

Earlier in his account, Raleigh gave God credit for the "great favor towards our nation, who by putting this purchase into our hands hath manifestly discovered those secret trades & Indian riches, which hitherto lay strangely hidden, and cunningly concealed from us. . . ." He went on to say that "whereof there was among some few of us some small and unperfect glimpse onely," the cargo of the *Madre de Dios* had turned that glimpse "into the broad light of full and perfect knowledge." Then with true seventeenth-century logic, he added, "Whereby it should seeme that the will of God for our good is . . . to have us communicate with them in those East Indian treasures, . . ."[3]

It was eight years, however, before Elizabeth agreed to charter "The Governour and Merchants of London Trading into the East Indies." Not until the thirty-first of December 1600, as almost the last act of her long and calculating reign, did the Virgin Queen launch the English East India Company into the economic waters of the world. At the

8) East India Company's coat-of-arms with 17th-century punning motto, *Deus Indicat.*

time, the Company, in full agreement with Raleigh's credit to divine guidance in the whole affair, chose as its motto *Deus Indicat,* a pun contrived in the seventeenth-century manner, prophetically to connect God's will with the future of India in the interest of the Company. The words, written on a ribbon, curved across the top of their coat-of-arms, which consisted of an escutcheon charged with Tudor roses, fleurs-de-lis, and three sailing ships on banded fields of gold and azure, supported on either side by azure sea lions, and crested with a skeletal globe. These heraldic symbols emblazoned across their banner proclaimed the Company's pride of origin and its hope of the future.

However, the high hopes held by Company sponsors in England were tempered by the facts in India, half a world away. Both local pirates and the previously established Portuguese resented with force any intrusion into their eastern trade monopoly. And the Dutch, who by 1602 had consolidated their scattered trade concessions in the East into The United East India Company of the Netherlands, fought furiously to keep and to enlarge their holdings. During the first three or four decades of the seventeenth century, of any "twenty ships sent out [from England] . . . scarce one returned" unless the Company "sent three ships to protect one."[4]

In spite of such formidable opposition, usually armed, by 1603 the

English succeeded in getting their first toehold in the East Indies at Bantam on Java. Gifts to the native king of "5 or 6 doz. knives" and "one brass standard with weights, and 2 iron beams" secured the advantage, with the addition of three large looking-glasses, three "chambletts" —probably "camlets," garments made of English woolens of that name —plus some loops and buttons of silk and gold "to the value of 10£."[5]

But it wasn't until 1610 that the English East India Company was able to establish itself on the mainland at Surat, the most northwesterly harbor on the west coast of India. There it erected its first "factory"— company parlance for a combination countinghouse, warehouse, treasury, and residence. On the entire Malabar Coast, Surat was the only adequate harbor not previously usurped by the Portuguese or the Dutch. The next year Masulipatam on the Coromandel coast, the east coast of India, became the first English settlement on the Bay of Bengal.

Harbors on the Bay of Bengal were little more than shallow variations in the coastline. Top-heavy, kettle-bottomed European trading ships could approach no closer to them than a hazardous roadstead in the open sea. Racing against the time when the monsoon would sweep out of the southwest, native surf-riders shuttled their little boats heaped high with trade goods across the intervening tricky waters. If they were lucky, for half a year they could collect cargo for the foreigners; the other six months furies of rain and ocean water hurled everything on the sea into oblivion.

Such was the location of Madraspatam, about halfway up the east coast of India, only a slight improvement over the earlier station of Masulipatam. In the 1630s, Madraspatam had also been deliberately bartered for in trade, and with diplomacy. Deftly straddling the worlds of East and West, the dark-skinned Muslim potentate of the now vanished Kingdom of Golconda had requested as his share of the transaction—among other things—a lightweight suit of armor, ten yards each of scarlet, crimson, and violet satin, one pair of globes to show him where he reigned, and a "perspective glass" that would add depth and some reality to the flat little engraved "views" from which he imagined the world beyond his realm.[6] The English, too, had bargained well, for even today "Golconda" is still synonymous with "riches." This was true even more so then. By 1640 they had fortified the town whose name they shortened to "Madras," and which as "Fort St. George" was valued at £6000 on the books of the Company in 1649. But its price was beyond figures, for it was to dominate the settlements and the future trade of the Coromandel Coast on the east side of India.

At this point, forty years after Queen Elizabeth with hope and trepidation had launched the East India Company, it had mighty little to show for its years of exhilarations and disappointments, for the bloodshed and triumphs, barter, booty, and homesickness. In India, the natives refused to accommodate themselves or their products to English needs. And in England, under Charles I, times were becoming so politically uncertain that merchants hesitated to stock luxuries, especially

9) Another eastern potentate was the King of Candy (Ceylon), Fimala Derura Suriada, called "Colombo," shown here with the Dutch Admiral Joris van Spilbergen. C. 1602. From the abridged Latin edition of Johann Theodore Bry's *Indiae Orientalis Pars Septima; Navigationes duas . . . ,* 1606.

silks, calicoes, and indigo. The situation became so acute that share-holders in the Company had to accept their profits in cloves, cinnamon, and indigo, or wait for their cash until the cargo was slowly sold. Spices often had to find a foreign market. Pepper, for instance, could be traded in Italy for coral, which had to be carried back to India before it would realize the expected speculative profit of an average 90 percent. But calicoes were considered "now a dead commodity, neither linen drapers nor others offering reasonable prices for them."[7]

Only those few who had private contacts, such as Lady Haversly, enjoyed the luxury of receiving "free of freight 2 small cabinets and 10 pieces of calicoes sent her by her son-in-law."[8] And somehow, Lady Gerrard had collected a dinner service of porcelain which impressed John Evelyn,* just back from the Continent early in 1652, as "the most ample and richest collection of that curiosity in England."[9]

Such luxuries were the exceptions in these times. The rule for luxuries during the puritanical years that followed the death of Charles I, was the same as that for other symbols of the buried monarchy, expressed by Cromwell when he dissolved the Long Parliament and disposed of the mace with "take away that shining bauble there."[10] Yet it was for lack of a market for "baubles" that the East India trade almost expired. Silks and calicoes were replaced by sad-colored home-spun woolens, because, in the words of Cromwell's General Harrison, "gold and silver and worldly bravery did not become saints."[11] Not until 1657 did Cromwell see the necessity of strengthening the ailing Company, if for no other reason than that of keeping the Dutch from enlarging their eastern holdings. New stock was subscribed, a new charter signed, and the old incentive of quick, fat riches was revived.

Neither the Company nor England, however, had improved its financial standing by 1660, the year Charles II was restored to the throne. Finances and the rising power of the Dutch concerned each equally.

---

* *John Evelyn (1620–1706), a Cavalier, a Royalist, and a seventeenth-century "virtuoso," born to wealth and position, kept a diary for sixty-one years since he was twenty-one. During the Restoration, he was close to Charles II, served as a Commissioner of Trade and Plantations concerned with colonies and the West Indies, was a founder of the Royal Society, a friend of Pepys, "discovered" Grinling Gibbons, and submitted plans for the rebuilding of London after the Great Fire in friendly competition with Sir Christopher Wren.*

From Charles's point of view, the dowry of the Infanta of Portugal presented itself as a practical and timely solution, particularly since its monetary provision promised to be so generous.

As for the acquisition of Bombay, Charles probably never considered that an important reason for marrying Catherine of Braganza. Neither could Parliament see any startling advantage in its possession. But to the East India Company, Bombay was a matter of survival. For years they had envied the Portuguese the magnificent natural harbor of Bombay through which drained the finest products of India. In fact, the Company had even urged Cromwell to buy it for a price. But only those Englishmen who had adventured in the South Seas were able to recognize the inestimable value of Bombay—they and the Portuguese. It took three years and five men-of-war to persuade the deserted Portuguese governor of Bombay that his jewel of the Indian Ocean had been deeded to Charles II in 1662, along with a Portuguese bride.

After the transfer of Bombay, the Portuguese practically disappeared from the continent they had opened to European trade one hundred and fifty years before. Now it was the Dutch who proclaimed themselves "Lords of the Southern Seas," threatening confiscation to all competing commerce. In answer, the reactivated English East India Company was empowered by Charles II in 1676, to make war and peace, acquire troops, fortresses, and territory, and was even granted "full and free liberty, power and authority, from time to time, and at all times hereafter, to stamp and coin . . . monies"[12] in the trade empire they conjured out of the dowry of Catherine of Braganza.

CHAPTER THREE

"Politer" Living

"*A politer way of living, which passed to luxury and intolerable expense.*"—JOHN EVELYN, *February 4, 1685*

LEAVING behind them in Portsmouth the pealing bells and bonfires that celebrated their marriage, Charles II and Catherine processioned to London. The whole royal entourage had been unexpectedly delayed from starting as scheduled, Charles wrote to his Chancellor, "by reason that there is not cartes to be had to-morrow, to transporte all our guarde infantas, without which there is no stirring; so as you are not to expect me till Thursday night at Hamton Courte."[*1]

It was May 29, 1662, his thirty-second birthday, when Charles and his bride arrived there. Court and populace alike craned for a glimpse of the new foreign Queen and her "train of Portuguese ladies," whom Evelyn disparagingly described as possessed of "complexions olivader and sufficiently unagreeable." But it was those "monstrous fardingales,

---

* *Hampton Court, the royal residence, called by Evelyn (June 2, 1662), "as noble and uniform a pile, and as capacious as any Gothic architecture can have made it." It had been acquired by Cardinal Wolsey, and presented to Henry VIII in 1526 for a royal residence.*

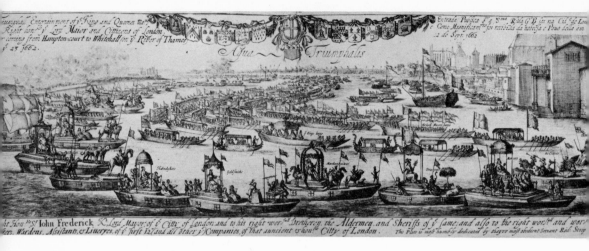

10) The Water Pageant on the Thames which escorted Catherine and Charles from Hampton Court to Whitehall, August 23, 1662. The King's Barge in the center, shaded by a plume-crested canopy, is surrounded by symbolically decorated floats of every guild of London. One of a set of seven engraved by Dirk Stoop.

or guard-enfantes," they insisted on wearing, that emphasized their outlandishness; for farthingales—the rigid hoop skirts of Queen Elizabeth's day—had been out of fashion in England for at least a half century.

Even Catherine was so attired. In spite of that, Evelyn thought "She was yet of the handsomest countenance of all the rest, and, though low of stature, prettily shaped." He frankly admired her "languishing and excellent eyes," but with the same glance noticed "her teeth wronging her mouth by sticking a little too far out." Loyally he added, "for the rest, lovely enough."[2]

By mid-August, talk of farthingales and duennas was replaced by the excitement of the water pageant on the Thames, staged to conduct Charles and his Queen up river from Hampton Court to Whitehall. On the twenty-third, bursts of fireworks started early to compete with welcoming royal salutes in smothering the catchy melodies of stringed music that mingled with the rumble of impatient humanity agape on the river banks. High above the din, crushed between the satins and laces of privileged courtiers and their ladies on the roof of the Banqueting House of Whitehall,* Samuel Pepys watched the colorful spectacle. A thousand or more barges and boats in competitive "holiday dress" crowded the river for as far as Pepys could see, with hardly a shimmer of water between them.

Through this jam, John Evelyn sailed his own scow, newly built for the occasion. So close did he come to the royal "antique-shaped open vessel" that he could almost touch Catherine seated next to Charles under the "canopy of cloth of gold, made in the form of a cupola, supported with high Corinthian pillars, wreathed with flowers, festoons and garlands." In Evelyn's opinion, "it far exceeded all the Venetian Bucentoras [gala gondolas], &c., on Ascension [Day], when they espouse the Adriatic."[3] That festival commemorates Venice's freedom from encircling pirates in A.D. 1000, and it is still celebrated today.

Nothing like this, though, had been seen in England for decades. A whole generation had grown to manhood in ignorance of even the most normal pleasures of life. Under the puritanical regime of Cromwell, plays, cards, and dancing were prohibited, traditional May Day ceremonies forbidden, and even Christmas was proclaimed a fast day, although no man-made rules could successfully suppress all celebration of Christmas. The return of a pleasure-loving King to the throne suddenly swung the pendulum far to the side of all sorts of luxuries. Years of denial had built up a hunger in the people, not alone for entertainment, but also for comforts of the body and things pleasant to the eye. Merchants and craftsmen of all kinds began to flourish under the accelerated demand for new and beautiful furbishings. Things from the East were especially sought after, as they spasmodically appeared in the markets; and their exotic shapes, textures, and colors influenced domestic goods with increasing frequency.

When Catherine of Braganza came to England, little more than a coat-of-arms was left the East India Company after sixty years of discouragements at home and abroad. Of all the villages they had fought and died for, only Surat and Madraspatam still tied the Company to India. As for cargoes, the richest ever seen by this generation of Englishmen were those taken as prizes from the Dutch.

* From here Charles I had stepped through one of the floor-length windows to the platform of his scaffold in 1649. Whitehall was originally planned by Inigo Jones in 1619 as part of a royal palace, but never more than the Banqueting House was finished. It still stands in London.

"Pepper scattered through every chink, you trod upon it; and in cloves and nutmegs I walked above the knees: whole rooms full," marveled Samuel Pepys after inspecting the holds of one of their captured "India ships." There he saw, it seemed to him, "the greatest wealth lie in confusion that a man can see in the world." Not only were there spices, but also "silk in bales, and boxes of copper-plate," one of which Pepys opened in his disbelief. Such things were rare in England in the 1660s, and in proportion were fully as valuable as the eight bags of diamonds and rubies and other precious stones taken that day from around the neck of the Dutch vice-admiral in command. Later Pepys could not shake the wonderment that possessed him, for he ended his entry with the statement: "Having seen this, which was as noble a sight as ever I saw in my life."[4]

This multiplicity of exotic delights was the real wealth tucked between the lines of Catherine's dowry treaty. Slowly it now began to trickle into England, these riches that for one hundred and fifty years had been adventured for in the East by Catherine's exploring Portuguese forebears.

For centuries before Vasco da Gama ever reached Calicut, the rich beauty of the East had been familiar to those of the Iberian Peninsula. Oriental trade goods had flowed across the Mediterranean into Spain and Portugal alike, through the ports of Venice and Genoa, from Constantinople, or directly from Gombroon on the Persian Gulf, terminus of cross-Asia camel caravans. When the trade routes of the world shifted, and Portugal by accident and design pioneered an empire in the East while Spain exploited the Americas, the cultures of the Orient continued to add exotic flair, as well as spice, to the peninsula of Hispania. Then during the sixteenth century, in the wake of an unnatural political alliance, the flavor of the East began to travel north into the Netherlands along the Spanish military corridor of Europe.

A strategic succession of marriages and deaths had already united much of Europe under Charles V, when in 1519 he succeeded his paternal grandfather, Maximilian of Habsburg, as Emperor of the Holy Roman Empire. Born in Ghent in 1500, Charles came naturally by his inheritance of that part of the Netherlands that became known as "Spanish." Then on the death of his maternal grandfather in 1516, he also fell heir to the Spain of Ferdinand and Isabella, together with all of Spain's American possessions. When in 1566 Charles V abdicated his enormous responsibilities scattered around the globe, the Spanish part of his empire fell to his son Philip II, he of the Spanish Armada, who was briefly husband to Mary Tudor, sister of England's first Queen Elizabeth. For the better part of the sixteenth century, Spain struggled to hold on to all the loosely federated provinces of the Netherlands and to that end beat a path north over Europe by land, as well as by way of the sea. Nevertheless, in 1579, several northern Protestant states managed to break away, and formed the confederacy of Holland.

For Portugal, however, one hundred years of growth and prosperity slipped, in 1581, into sixty ignominious years of "captivity" to Spain, furthering the similarity of their cultures. But Portuguese trade with the East Indies through Lisbon on the Atlantic, continued to enrich Portuguese arts and crafts, as well as her coffers.

It wasn't until 1640 that the disputed throne of Portugal was reclaimed by Catherine's father, the 8th Duke of Braganza. Of the handful of great powers at that time, only Charles I of England would recognize him as King, and that only in political spite of Rome, Spain, and half of Europe. Forty-eight uneasy years later, after Catherine had long been Queen of England, Spain at last conceded defeat and grudgingly signed a treaty of peace with Portugal, recognizing her as a sovereign power.

Pearls, porcelain, folding fans, and monkeys; silks, rugs, perfumes, and calicoes—these had always found a ready acceptance for themselves, whether in Portugal or in England. In fact, in certain European circles, they were as well known as in their countries of origin. In addition to these, however, Catherine, her dowry, and the hundreds of Portuguese artisans that followed her to England brought to the beauty-starved English a fascinating amalgamation of designs, materials, and customs divergent in origin, yet oddly blended together through generations of use in Portugal. In England, this foreign influence shaped the turn of a chair leg, popularized the use of woven cane, made fashionable a cup of tea, and further dramatically enriched English living in countless unexpected ways.

"To this excess of superfluity we were now arrived," wrote John Evelyn when shown the newly imported cabinets and porcelains of a friend, adding almost with embarrassment, "and that not only at Court,

11) English Restoration chair. A walnut cane chair with spiral turnings, "Spanish feet" or "Braganza toes," and mermaids holding up the royal crown. 1660–70.

but almost universally, even to wantonness and profusion."[5] Actually, Catherine's dowry was beginning rapidly to enrich even the least Englishman's living. By 1682, Evelyn was happy to record his own good fortune: "I sold my East India adventure of £250 principal for £750 . . . , after I had been in that company twenty-five years, being extra-ordinary advantageous, by the blessing of God."[6]

Much had happened in those twenty-five years Evelyn had held his "East India adventure," the twenty-five years since Cromwell had reorganized the old East India Company. Probably the improvement most noticeable to every Londoner was the new façade on the old quarters of the Company in Leadenhall Street, erected in 1661 in celebration of the coronation of Charles II. The minutes of the Court of Committees on March 20, 1661, queried "what preparations to make against the Coronation to represent the Companies loyall gratitude to His Majesty and how to beautify the front of this house."[7] By April 17 the work was finished, for Samuel Pepys "saw the picture of the ships and other things this morning set up before the East Indy House," and called them "well done." In fact, East India House remained so decorated until 1726.

It was, however, especially after Charles in 1668 turned Catherine's dowry gift of Bombay over to the Company, that its fortunes substantially and obviously prospered. Company minutes acknowledge the transfer by committing "the Company, their successors, and assigns [to] render and pay yearly unto His majesty, His Heirs, and Successors, ten pounds in gold of lawful money of England . . . as a rent and acknowledgment to His Majesty for the said island."[8] Only then was the Company able to give the truculent Dutch serious competition. Stations were established, residence warehouses (called "factories" in the East) were built, and by 1690 the port city of Calcutta had materialized out of the swamps.

Early in the history of the East India Company, its doctor at Surat had cured the favorite daughter of Shah Jehan, sentimental builder of the Taj Mahal. In gratitude, the Shah granted the Company a marshy spot the natives called Chutanutty (with a hard "Ch"), on a fork near the mouth of the Ganges. Even while English tongues pronounced it into "Calcutta," English enterprise built it into a port that was one day to rival that of London.

12) The old East India House façade. From a shop bill of William Overley, Joiner in Leadenhall Street, as reproduced in *Gentleman's Magazine,* London, December 1784.

13) K'ang Hsi in the early 18th century, toward the end of his reign.

Still, the rest of Asia remained adamant to East India Company overtures. "Concerning the Trade of China," an Englishman on the spot wrote to the Company directors in 1627, "three things are especially made known unto the World.

The One is, the abundant trade it [China] affordeth.
The Second is, that they admit no stranger into their country.
The Third is, that Trade is as Life unto the Vulgar, which in remote parts they will seek and accommodate, with Hazard of all they have."[9]

All through the seventeenth century, that "Third" point sent brash sea captains bluffing or forcing their way into Chinese ports. Courteous, firm Chinese indifference that flared into hostility when forced, even more than sea pirates and the entrenched Portuguese, made direct trade with China an illusion. Only on Taiwan (Formosa) and at Bantam in Java could Englishmen barter with Chinese merchants. Not until K'ang Hsi, the first Manchu emperor of China, saw disadvantages in Chinese isolation was foreign trade with the mainland tolerated. It was 1662 when K'ang Hsi became emperor of a conquered China, the same year Charles II married Catherine of Braganza, half a world away. Yet, it was not until 1699 that K'ang Hsi experimentally opened the port of Canton to the English, possibly as much to give the entrenched Portuguese some competition as out of curiosity of what the English had to offer in the line of trade.

Even then, conditions were still difficult, according to the supercargo of the *Macclesfield,* the first English ship to trade successfully at Canton. "Ye* many troubles & vexations we have mett wth from these subtile Chineese—whose principalls allow them to cheat, & y^r dayly practise therein have made y^m dextrus at it—I am not able to expresse at y^s time; and how ever easie others may have represented ye trade of China, nether I nor my Assistants have found it so, for every day produces new troubles, but I hope y^t a little time will put an end to them all."[10]

The trade situation was still worse with Japan. With the eviction of the Portuguese in 1638, all foreign ships had been forbidden Japanese

* *The "Y" of "Ye" and of the raised-letter words is to be read as "th."*

ports. The same year, however, by persistently disclaiming with words and deeds any affiliation with the hated Portuguese, the Dutch were grudgingly allowed a meager trading toehold on the artificial island of Deshima, which was tied to Nagasaki by a bridge. On this bit of fill, barely three hundred paces in any direction, they carried on trade under humiliating conditions for almost two centuries. But when the English asked for similar trading rights, the Japanese remembered the old fury they felt for the Portuguese. According to the report made by the Company, Japan replied to their overtures that "since our King [Charles II] was married with the daughter of Portugal, their enemy, they could not admit us to have any trade, and for no other reason."[11]

Catherine met with hardly a warmer welcome in England. "The new Queen gave but little additional brilliancy to the court, either in her person, or in her retinue"[12] was the opinion of the gay, young, exiled French Count de Gramont, who had had the temerity to pay court to one of Louis XIV's favorites. Pepys was kinder. He thought that though Catherine "be not very charming, yet she hath a good, modest, and innocent look, which is pleasing."[13] That "innocent look" was indeed a novelty at a court where manners extended liberally beyond even the accepted freedom of the times. It had attracted Charles when he first saw Catherine's betrothal miniature, but it was not enough to keep him faithful to her. Yet even while he acted on the assumption that "God would not damn a man for a little irregular pleasure,"[14] that pristine quality of hers kept bringing him back to her side.

From being "bred hugely retired," Catherine had been suddenly exposed to the outrages of a young court that reveled in the luxury of reaction to a generation of bigoted restraint. Every waking hour, both she and Charles were exposed to the prying eyes of curious subjects. As a matter of custom and privilege, the royal couple's dressing and undressing, their eating, their pleasures, and their troubles were public entertainment. A look, a smile, a shrug were given as many meanings as there were tongues in the audience.

Through a year of this, Catherine painfully adjusted herself to the free and intimate manners of her adopted home. Pepys thought she had "spirit enough" when she ignored Charles's "little irregular pleasures" —"seeing that she do no good by taking notice . . ."[15] About the same time the Count de Gramont described the Queen as "a woman of

14) Royal marriage charger of Lambeth delft, marked C R and K R, made to commemorate the marriage of Charles II and Catherine of Braganza in 1662. Diameter, 16¾ inches. Reproduced from *The Connoisseur.*

sense, who used all her endeavours to please the king, by that kind obliging behavior which her affection made natural to her. . . ."[16] But neither of these gentlemen ever suspected that Catherine had placed her problem in more capable hands, for she had presented a portrait of her husband to Syon Abbey in Devon, with the request that the nuns there pray for him. To this day Charles still hangs on the wall of their Great Hall smiling his half-satiric smile amidst rows of English saints with solemn faces, as if he were amused by the whole situation.

As for Catherine, she soon grew "briske" and "debonnaire," and Pepys was pleased to see that she began to "play like other ladies, and is quite another woman from what she was."[17] Evident, too, was the fact that England was changing, and for quite a number of reasons—many of which had traveled halfway around the world in the holds of rolling East India ships.

Cottons from India

THE farthingales that delayed Charles and Catherine's arrival at Hampton Court had been traditional Portuguese court costume as long as anyone could remember. Made of the richest silk damask, heavy enough to stand alone even without their cone-shaped foundation cages, these badges of royalty swept the floor evenly all around, because it was indecent to show the feet. But in their very modesty and rigidity, even in their material, they had been long out of fashion in England and now made fine targets for cruel ridicule.

At first, Catherine had persisted in wearing her farthingale "for the dignity of Portugal." Her ladies, "for the most part, old, and ugly, and proud," made her believe that if she would "neither learn the English language, nor use their habit, nor depart from the manners and fashions of her own country in any particulars: . . . she would quickly induce the English ladies to conform to her majesty's practise."[2] They promptly found out otherwise.

Within weeks Charles made short work of the "six frights, who called themselves maids-of-honour,"[3] and sent them all back to Portugal. On a fine day soon after, Pepys saw Catherine riding in the Park in "a white laced waistcoate and a crimson . . . pettycoate," holding hands with Charles, "her hair dressed *à la négligence,* mighty pretty."[4] Trains were then worn at court on "a sort of fantastic nightgown, fastened with a single pin";[5] but Pepys heard "talk that the Queen hath a great mind to alter her fashion, and to have the feet seen; which she loves mightily."[6]

In the rest of England away from the court, the gentry wore "fine English brocades and Venetians," according to a contemporary pamphlet. "Common Traders' wives [were clothed] with slight silk Damasks, . . . country Farmers' wives and other good country dames with worsted Damasks, flowered Russels and flowered Callimancoes, the meanest of them in plain worsted stuffs."[7] Worsteds, russels, and callimancoes were English woolens, sheared, spun, and woven in tiny thatched cottages that clustered at the crossroads of the meadows where sheep had grazed since Roman times.

For almost as long, wool had been the staple of England's economy. When the merchants of London began trading "into" the East Indies, they were required to carry not less than one tenth of their outbound cargo in "the growth, produce, or manufacture of the Kingdom." From

15) The simple costume of the Commonwealth persisted in the Provinces until near the end of the 17th century. Engraved by Richard Gaywood after W. Hollar, 1654.

first to last, English wool found its way to the East as broadcloth, scarletts, perpetuanoes, camletts, says, or shalloons. The names changed through the years, as the goods bartered for varied with the port and the fashion. Even though Company factors in India complained bitterly that they found no market for wool in the steaming tropics, the fat red woolsack* on the presiding seat of the House of Lords would have its tithe of trade.

Only at Surat, the first place in India where the Company succeeded in establishing a factory, was wool cloth in temporary demand. There the local King of Jahangir "maketh with the same, covertures for certain pretty castles that are wont to be fastened upon the backs of his elephants, wherein his women ride when he goeth abroad for solace sake some few miles from his seat of residence; . . ."[8] After the king had covered all the litters and saddles used by his women, his need for English woolens ceased, and the factors had to find other inducements with which to barter for calicoes.

Until the 1640s, plain calicoes were included in every cargo from India. Called derebauds, broderas, dorbellas, et cetera, in their native land, they were all generically calicoes to Englishmen, whether they came from the neighborhood of Calicut or not. In England, they were used for bedclothes and as clothing for the poor, instead of the more expensive linen from Holland. Then suddenly calicoes were "a dead commodity." The dissensions that led to the hanging of Charles I and the bitter years of the Commonwealth that followed were "troublesome tymes, when all trade and commerce in this kingdome is almost fallen to the ground through our owne unhappie divisions at home, unto which the Lord in mercie put a good end . . ."[9]

No sooner had Catherine set foot in England with Bombay in her dowry than the directors of the East India Company, their courage renewed, sent out "patterns of Chints . . . to cause a considerable quantity to be made of those Workes."[10] Itinerant calico weavers wandered back to Surat, and to Masulipatam on the Coromandel Coast—where the best painters of cottons plied their art—and there under the shade of a tamarind or mango tree they again set up their looms at sunrise each morning.

---

* *A thick cushion stuffed with raw wool and covered in red cloth, symbol of wool's importance to English economy, on which to this day the Lord Chancellor sits when presiding over the House of Lords.*

16) Hindu weaver at his portable loom tied between two trees, in the tradition of the East. From an old woodcut.

The Hindi word *chint* teases the imagination far more than its mundane translation of "spotted or variegated." Yet fine, closely woven calico was "spotted," if you will, with sprigs of nameless flowers, seed pods, vines, and trailing grasses; and "variegated" in shades of blue, red, green, and yellow, in an arrangement so natural that when draped on the wearer it swayed with the life of a breeze.

The painted calicoes, which particularly caught the Occidental fancy, were those the early Portuguese had called *pintados,* their word for "paintings." In India, pintados were the picture-painted calico panels that natives hung in honor of a guest to compliment his special interest or accomplishment, or simply to imitate nature in their homes. The one John Evelyn admired in 1665 was "full of figures great and small, prettily representing sundry trades and occupations of the Indians, with their habits."[11] The commercial minds of Company factors named them *palampores,* a Hindi-Persian combination meaning "bedcovers," and the directors in London ordered that more should be painted with "branches." To encourage their sale in England, it was experimentally specified in the 1680s that the "grounds [were] to be green, purple, red and some white, . . . with variety of painting, curious and lively brisk colours . . ."[12]

At painting palampores, the natives of Masulipatam in the pocket kingdom of Golconda were hereditary masters. Other communities developed their own techniques, but the palampores of Masulipatam were

17) An Indian palampore of painted cotton from the Coromandel Coast. A coverlet or hanging in the so-called "tree-of-life" design. Late 17th century.

invariably mentioned by name in the correspondence, invoices, and inventories of the time. Generations of trial and error had bred in the natives a skill with colors unknown to the West. Using the natural materials at hand with professional assurance, they conditioned raw calico for painting by soaking folded lengths of the cotton cloth in powdered *cadou* fruit and buffalo milk. Then it was beaten countless times with a tamarind club until so smooth that the painter's brush might glide unhindered across its polished surface and the color could not stray beyond the hair-thin outlines of the pattern. Designs as old as time or as new as the East India Company were "pounced" on the treated calico with powdered charcoal through pinpricked paper, and the outlines sparingly drawn in black or red only enough to guide the color painters.[13]

In every ancient culture, pictures preceded words in the art of story-

18) A painted India cotton coverlet with pairs of native birds flitting and roosting in a "tree" of bamboo. c. 1680.

telling. In the India touched by European trade, the natives recorded their customs, habits, and history on polychrome palampores and twined the lush foliage, flower, and seed of their plains and their forests through background and border. Every detail had some meaning. But in England were preferred those palampores that grew a fantastic tree on a mound of conventionalized hillocks and reached to the heavens loaded with color. Even though in 1662 the Company sent out "patterns of chints" for the natives to copy, the giant blossoms and outsized leaves they created were drawn with imagination and license out of a tropical nature which was far more generous than the north temperate zone of England with its primroses and daisies.

The tree-of-life on palampores, in all its exotic beauty and asym-

19) Chinese bronze lamp in ancient "tree-of-life" form. Han dynasty (206 B.C.–A.D. 220).

metrical grace, was a synthesis of many trees of the ancient eastern fertility cults, even of that tree in the garden of Eden from which Adam was expelled, "lest he put forth his hand and take also of the tree of life, and eat, and live for ever."[14] Few Englishmen knew its symbolism even though they were charmed by its spell. If the natives understood what they painted, it bore the stamp of their mysticism; otherwise painting palampores was just another means of earning food for the rainy season.

Blue was applied first—not painted on, but resist-dyed with indigo. Using an iron pencil wrapped round with a saturated ball of hair that oozed liquid wax down through the split point of the pencil, wax painters covered every bit of cloth not to be blue or green. Their strong hands then pressed the wax deep into every fiber, as they worked the cloth across the round bottom of a brass kettle, warm from the heat of the sun. Next, special indigo dyers took over and practiced their tricky business in secret. Several days later the cloth, now blue in the right places, was boiled and boiled again to melt out all the wax, bleached with sheep droppings, washed by the river's edge, folded, and beaten dry against a flat stone, much as a blacksmith smites his anvil with a hammer.[15]

For shades of red, the calico was again soaked in a concoction of buffalo milk and vigorously beaten dry. Little children then touched the color on flower petals and butterfly wings in the design with a bit of rag stuck into a piece of split bamboo, after they had squeezed out the excess red dye with their fingers. Washed, bleached as before, and rinsed again, the painted cotton was folded to convenient size and once more beaten twenty, thirty times, further to mangle smooth its fibers.[16]

Yellow, least dependable of colors, was the last to be painted on the bright spots for its own sake and over blue wherever green was wanted. With sour whey, or a solution of India's all-purpose cow dung, native painters lengthened its fickle life. Washed with soap and water, bleached and rinsed again, folded and beaten to a finish, no subsequent use could possibly fade an India painted calico.[17] Not until the eighteenth century was the ancient technique supplemented with block printing to keep up with the demand, for the "painting of chintzes proceeds in the most leisurely manner in the world, . . . similar to the crawling of snails, which appear to make no headway."[18]

20) "Homme en Robe de Chambre." Man in a *banyan* worn over his shirt and breeches. The fur cap, or an embroidered one, covered a man's shaved head indoors, when without a wig. Engraved by Nicolas Bonnart, 1676.

In London, at Company candle auctions, broad and narrow chintz, baftas, and derebauds appeared regularly among the twenty-odd India cottons knocked down to the highest bidder. In the Blue, Pepper, or Calico Warehouse, twice a year, when the trade ships were in, interested merchants frantically bid for a lot each time one measured inch of candle flamed, sputtered, and burned out. Only saltpeter for the Crown was sold by contract, as "it was not honourable nor decent for the King to buy at the candle, as other common persons did."[19]

By the end of the 1660s, cotton yarn headed the April and October "Court of Sales" list, followed by pepper which previously had been of prime importance—Malabar, Jambi, Quilon, and "scummings and dust of Pepper"—once in 1640, even "light, stalky, stony, wet, dry and mouldy pepper." Then in exotic variety followed "flat and round" indigo, sugar, green ginger, myrrh, turmeric, cowries, saltpeter, seed-lac, etc., and in 1669, the first "theapots," 130 of them which brought 30 shillings each at the last gasp of the candle.[20]

Year after year the lists of East India goods grew longer, more valuable and choice. From covering four or five pages in the Court Books of the 1660s, they extended to as many as twenty-seven in 1675. It was then that "cotton gowns," "Japan gowns," "painted calicoes," and even "calico waistcoats" first appeared, and the next year, "palampores." In previous years, such special cottons had been brought to England by "servants" of the Company as tokens or as "private trade," and had pleased a relative or paid off a favor, as is still the custom in our time. In that way Mrs. Pepys received her "Japan gowne" in December 1663,[21] but a "very noble parti-coloured Indian" one her husband returned, because he felt its value of 12 or 15 pounds was far too little for his past services to the donor—"I expect at least 50£ of him."[22]

As for palampores, by 1680, they were already sufficiently popular as bedcovers for the Company to risk an order of "100 Suits of painted Curtains and vallances [for bed-draperies] of Several Sorts and Prices, . . . but none too dear, nor any overmean in regard you know our Poorest people in England lye without any Curtains or Vallances and our richest in Damask, etc. . . ."[23] The next year, the London office wrote Surat "about Chints . . . you cannot imagine what a vast number of them would sell here . . . 200,000 of all sorts in a year will not be too much for this Markett."[24] By the time that order had been received in India, executed at native snail's pace, and possibly three years later delivered back in London, again halfway around the globe, chintz had "become the weare of ladyes of the greatest quality, which they wear on the outside of Gowns Mantuoes which they line with velvet and cloth of gold."[25]

Mantuoes were gowns worn open down the front to show a flash of elaborate petticoat. Related by name to Italy, which had faced East long before England was aware of the Orient, they were related in shape to "Indian gownes." Within one generation, mantuoes developed into an outer mantle, while Indian gowns remained *négligé* through a long life as "nightgowns" or "banyans." In India these loose-flowing cotton wrappers were the working costumes of "banians," the native clerks of Company factors. In England, they fitted the prevailing mood of undress, when "fashionables" received their callers in bed and the latest whim was to be painted in an Indian gown, as was Pepys in 1666— a gown he had "hired to be drawn in."[26]

As to when Catherine and Charles wore their Indian gowns, no one has hinted, but it is recorded that in 1684 there was an "Indian-gown maker" to the King named Robert Croft, and Mrs. Mandove was "Indian-gown maker" to the Queen.[27] The free naturalistic patterns of painted calicoes that glowed fresher with each washing appealed to a society long upholstered in formal, conventional, repetitive designs. Contemporary writers, however, never failed to be amazed at how fast and far chintz and calicoes had risen within their memory, when at first they "were only made use of for carpets, quilts, etc., and to clothe children, and ordinary people, . . ."[28] Fashions usually moved in the reverse order, but painted cottons were the exception. By the time Catherine left Whitehall in 1685, even the marble walls of the Queen's bathroom were hung with "India stuffs." Class had been no barrier to their charms.

Wool was now definitely out of fashion. "The general fansie of the people runs upon East India goods to that degree that the chints and painted calicoes . . . become now the dress of our ladies, . . . which but a few years before, their chambermaids would have thought too ordinary for them; . . . Nor was this all, but it crept into our houses, our closets, and bedchambers; curtains, cushions, chairs, and at last, beds themselves, were nothing but callicoes or Indian stuffs; and in short, almost everything that used to be made of wool or silk, . . . was supplied by the Indian trade."[29] That trade, which had been inaugurated primarily to vend English wool abroad, had crept back and stolen the home market. Entrenched wool interests screamed for legislative protection.

Torn between two powerful factions, Parliament compromised in 1678 by decreeing that all corpses be wrapped in woolen shrouds. After all, there were always many dead and their protesting voices died with them. All except Alexander Pope's *Narcissa:*

> "*Odious! in woollen! 'twould a saint provoke,*"
> *Were the last words that poor Narcissa spoke;*
> "*No, let a charming chintz and Brussels lace*
> *Wrap my cold limbs and shade my lifeless face:*
> *One would not, sure, be frightful when one's dead—*
> *And, Betty, give this cheek a little red.*"[30]

In spite of governmental prohibitions, cottons from India continued in high esteem, "from the greatest gallants to the meanest Cook

Maids."[31] In another attempt to help the wool industry, Parliament in 1700 even ruled that buttons and buttonholes were to be worked in wool instead of in silk. It went so far as to prohibit the importation of Chinese wrought silks, and finally, the importation of the popular India cottons—except those marked for re-export. So now the East India Company sold chintz and calico to the colonies, and adventurers "re-exported" the forbidden merchandise into up-country harbors of England or smuggled it onto some lonely beach. From there, peddlers carried packs of contraband goods into every village and hamlet. They only avoided such weaving towns as Spitalfields and Norwich, for there mobs of unemployed weavers—both of silk and wool—marched through the streets under banners of torn calico gowns, wrecked the stock of calico merchants, and threw disintegrating *aqua fortis* at anyone dressed in chintz.

21) Calico printing in England. The outlines of the design were stamped with wool blocks; the colors brushed in by hand. From John Barrow's *Supplement to the New & Universal Dictionary of Arts and Sciences,* 1754.

"Fashion is truly termed a witch; the dearer and scarcer any com
modity, the more the mode,"[32] philosophized a wool growers' pamphlet. Nothing could sell wool at home. So on December 27, 1703, the
Methuen Treaty was signed with Portugal, whereby English manufactures, especially wool cloth, enjoyed encouragingly low duties in Portugal. In exchange, England granted similar concessions to Portuguese
oranges and port. Appreciably little cloth was moved; but from then
on, the English drank port instead of claret, and further cemented their
friendship with Portugal.

Paid pamphleteers, including Daniel Defoe, continued to agitate, and
"foreign trumpery" found itself again legislated against. This time
the law extended to any kind of use made of painted calicoes after
December 25, 1722. For the next fifty-two years, not even cottons

22) David Garrick's bedroom furniture made by Haig and Chippendale in
1771, painted pale yellow with dark green chinoiserie decorations. The bed
is dressed in its original "tree-of-life" palampores. C. 1775.

printed in England could be worn or used for any sort of household decoration, on threat of a 5-pound fine to the wearer and 20-pound fine on him who sold the goods.

In the case of David Garrick, the actor, as presumably in many others, outright confiscation was the penalty. With the courage of a desperate spouse, Garrick asked the help of the Secretary of the Customs, for the return of his wife's forfeited bed curtains.

"Not Rachel, weeping for her children, could show more sorrow than Mrs. Garrick. Not weeping for her children for children she has none— nor, indeed, for her husband—thanks be to the humour of the times, she can be as philosophical upon that subject as her betters. —What does she weep for then? Shall I dare tell you? —It is for the loss of the chintz bed and curtains. The tale is short, and is as follows:—

"I have taken some pains to oblige the gentlemen of Calcutta, by sending them plays, scenes, and other services in my way; in return they have sent me Madeira, and poor Rachel the unfortunate chintz . . . She had prepared paper, chairs, &c. for this favourite token of Indian Gratitude. But, alas! all human felicity is frail! No care having been taken on my wife's part, and some treachery being exerted against her, it was seized,—the very bed,

> '*By the coarse hands of filthy dunghill villians,*
> *And thrown among the common lumber.*'

"If you have the least pity for a distressed Female,—any regard for her Husband, for he has had a sad time of it, . . . you may put your finger and thumb to the business, and take the thorn out of poor Rachel's side."[33]

That the Secretary did immediately, for the next day he wrote Garrick, "the wit of your letter flashes in my eyes, but the tale gives me distress." He said he had sent a "supplication" to an influential friend on the board "to prevail with the Harpies to come into a reasonable composition for the restitution of the chintz, and yet the Linnen Drapers and Cotton Printers and all that cursed Bourgoisie I fear will be as powerful as they are merciless . . ."[34]

Their power, however, had just run out with the statute. The bed, fully furnished with its tree-of-life palampore, was returned to Rachel.

It stands today in London's Victoria and Albert Museum, dressed in all its splendor of "Indian Gratitude."

By the time Rachel's bed was returned in 1775, the cotton interests were the rising economic force at the expense of both the India cotton trade and the English home-wool industry. Cotton was no stranger to the English economy. Cotton lint had been wick in the best wax candles for as long as pepper was known. Some cotton yarn, or "cotton wool" for English spinning, was included from the first in every East India cargo, until by 1669 it headed the biannual sales lists. English-spun cotton alone, however, wove too weak a fabric; but when combined with an Irish linen warp for strength, it produced a twill that gave some home competition to the hated imports.

Yet no amount of English ingenuity could imitate the riotously lovely India-painted calicoes by color-stamping English twill. So with needles threaded with fine crewel, the ladies of the Restoration embroidered their way around government prohibitions with surprising variations of the tree-of-life.

"Flowers, plants, and fishes, beasts, birds, flies, and bees,
Hills, dales, plains, pastures, skies, bees, rivers, trees . . ."[35]

23) Crewel embroidered "tree-of-life" bed and window hangings, in strong shades of blue-green and rust-red on a cotton and linen twill. English, late 17th century. Southeast Bedchamber, Palace, Colonial Williamsburg.

24) New England adaptation of the "tree-of-life" motif, sparingly embroidered in crewel in shades of rose, blue, green, and yellow. C. 1740. The spread originally belonged to Thomas Hancock of Boston, who left it to his nephew, John.

had long been stitched on valence and curtain by generations of English gentlewomen. With the Restoration, however, the dams of conformity had broken. Flowers now bloomed exotic and bolder. Only as crewel— the fine-spun, softly colored, worsted embroidery thread—did wool have any part in such decorations. Even here the fashion changed, for instead of wool embroidery, by the second quarter of the eighteenth century, silk-floss chain-stitch traced sophisticated versions of the still forbidden painted calicoes on linen or on twill.

Garments, on the other hand, were usually embroidered in silk in the design fashion of the time. Mrs. Delany, a chatty little lady who had many friends at court, described the dress the Duchess of Queensbury wore to some "doings at Norfolk House" early in 1741 as "white satin embroidered, the bottom of the petticoat *brown hills* covered with all sorts of weeds, and *every breadth* had *an old stump of a tree* that run up almost to the top of the petticoat, broken and ragged and worked with brown chenille, . . ." Such was the degeneration of the symbolic tree-of-life that but two or three generations before had brought the breath of far places into England. This eighteenth-century mangled version boasted "nastersians, ivy, honeysuckles, periwinkles, convolvuluses and all sorts of twining flowers" embroidered round the "old stump," which like "many of the leaves [was] finished with gold and . . . looked like the gilding of the sun."[36]

It was to be a long time before painted India cottons again came freely into England. The restrictions remained in force until 1774, when all bans were lifted, except those on corpses. They continued to be wrapped in woolens until 1814.

Wool had actually legislated itself out of fashion. Eighteenth-century ladies thought "no more of wolen stuff than . . . of an old almanac."[37] India cottons, however, were still as exciting as the day English privateers captured the Portuguese *Madre de Dios*. English cottons, by contrast, were still as narrow as the distance the shuttle could be thrown from a man's one hand to his other, and no finer than the indifferent yarn spun in country kitchens. Quality had mattered little until competition from the East threatened the English weaver's survival.

The continued challenge posed by the three-yard width of Indian palampores, led John Kay in 1733 to invent his "fly-shuttle," the first real improvement in generations of English weaving. With the jerk of a thong, Kay's shuttle could be projected across a widened loom, carrying the weft thread well beyond the customary stretch of a man's two arms.

In retrospect, the fly-shuttle is now considered to have launched the Industrial Revolution, but in 1733 it only earned for Kay the wrath of weavers and masters alike, who had been trained in the ancient weaving traditions of their grandfathers. From the first, Kay's invention was greeted with the fear and suspicion reserved only for great ideas, culminating in riots and bloodshed. Kay was driven from his home, and his fly-shuttle invention stolen, ironically enough by wool weavers who flatly refused him compensation. Some years later, the machine Kay was working on to improve the homespun quality of cotton was smashed by men gripped in the same unreasoning fear that occasionally still marks the advent of revolutionary improvements. Barely escaping

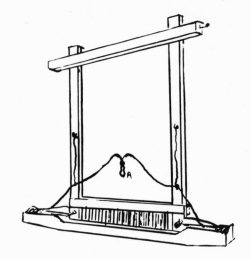

25) John Kay's "fly-shuttle." "A" marks handle attached to thongs that jerked the fly-shuttle across the loom at a sharp tug of the weaver's wrist.

with his life, Kay fled to France where he died disillusioned in poverty.

As gradually ever more pairs of hands were displaced by the clever gadgets and consolidated processes inspired by the superior cottons of India, the entire weaving industry—wool and silk alike—was caught in the pangs of readjustment. In the fall of 1763, several thousand journeyman weavers assembled in Spitalfields and vented their spleen on one of their masters, broke into his house "in a riotous and violent manner," and cut vast quantities of "rich" silk to ribbons. According to the account in *The Gentleman's Magazine,* they then "placed his effigy in a cart, with a halter about his neck, an executioner on one side, and a coffin on the other; and after drawing it thro' several streets, they hang'd it on a gibbet, then burnt it to ashes, and afterwards dispers'd."[38]

Nothing daunted, inspired fools throughout the century continued to weather the anguished protests of displaced handcraftsmen. One such was Richard Arkwright, who in 1771 climaxed years of inventive experiments with not only the first co-ordinated spinning mill, but the first one with machinery actually driven by waterpower. And in 1779, Samuel Crompton combined Arkwright's early horsepower spinning frame with the yet earlier multiple spinning "jenny" of James Hargreaves, the combination being subsequently dubbed a spinning "mule" by factory hands who had been bred on the farm. With this improvement, cotton could at last be spun in England fine and strong enough to weave calico competitive with that of India. And English calico could now even imitate the patterns and colors of India cottons, for in one revolution of its cylinder the newly invented, engraved copper, roller-printing machine printed as much fabric as formerly took four hundred and forty-eight separate applications of one hand-applied, carved wood block—probably as much as the entire output of an Indian family in a month.

Even though cotton seed from India was part of the equipment of the first Virginia Colony in 1616, little more than an occasional garden patch for family use was raised in America during the first century and a half. In the meantime, a gown of India-painted calico was crammed into the limited space of many a colonist's sea chest to pamper the feminine ego in the raw new world. When at the beginning of the eighteenth century, the East India Company found it had to circumvent government prohibitions on India cotton, it easily sold its "East India goods"—"chints, callicoes, and counterpanies"—in Boston, New York, Charles Town. By 1735, a calico printer advertised his skill in Boston, in "Prints of all sorts of Callicoes of several Colours to hold Washing."[39] And banyans called "night gowns" in the colonies, became so popular that in 1755 Harvard College had to pass a "law" forbidding their use on Commencement Day, to assure a dignified ceremony.[40]

Within the first decade after the end of the American Revolution, a young Englishman named Samuel Slater, run-away apprentice from Arkwright's spinning mill, unwittingly fathered New England's era of textile prosperity. Because the export of textile machines, even parts or plans, was a capital crime in England, Slater carried the plans for Arkwright's water-powered spinning frame—the cornerstone of the industry—in his head. Three years later, in 1793, the development of Eli Whitney's cotton gin promised sufficient raw material for the growing industrial economy and laid the foundations for the next century's empire of cotton plantations in the South. But even as England before it, the young nation faced the competition of India cottons, by then carried around the world in America's own East India ships, the "China Clippers."

Those were exciting times of national experiment and growth. Yet in many ways they echoed the revolution and expansion of Britain at the turn of the preceding century, when the impact of Catherine's dowry was turning the last vestiges of the Middle Ages into modern times.

26) Thomas Hubbard (1702–73), Harvard graduate, class of 1721, treasurer (1752–73) and benefactor of the college, Speaker of Massachusetts House of Representatives, and a member of the Governor's Council. Posed for John S. Copley in blue damask banyan and purple cap, 1767.

CHAPTER FIVE

East India Cane

"Cane-Chairs . . . gave so much satisfaction to all the
Nobility, Gentry and Commonalty of this Kingdom . . ."

—CANE CHAIR-MAKERS' PETITION[1]

THE Court of St. James's, in the early days of the Stuart Restoration when Catherine had just arrived in England as a bride, was torn between solid, old-fashioned English virtues and newly acquired, high-fashion French customs. The consoling French convention of supporting an assortment of personable mistresses was probably the most alien practice Charles had acquired during a lonesome unattached youth on the Continent. It was an addiction Catherine found hard to understand, a fact that the Chancellor, Edward Hyde, blamed on her tutors, who "had given her no better Information of the Follies and Iniquities of Mankind, of which He presumed the Climate from whence She came could have given more Instances, than this Cold Region would afford."[2]

However, the more practical ideas Charles had gathered at the courts of Europe mingled well with things brought to England by Catherine in her dowry and combined to accelerate the Stuart Restoration into a "politer way of living which passed to luxury and intolerable expense"[3] within one generation. Anything foreign was desirable; anything "exotically" foreign was irresistible and high fashion. Yet of all the innova-

27) English Restoration chair of cane and walnut, with spiral turnings and a crown in crest and stretcher. C. 1680.

tions of the period, no one single piece of furniture shows the amalgamation of cultures quite as plainly as does the regal "Restoration" chair.

A chair, in any period, has combined within its contours volumes of history—social, economic, and political. It stands as a symbol of its time. By its very existence it bespeaks authority, since for centuries the chair was only for the master or his guest, while women, children, and retainers sat upon stools or benches. By its very size and shape, a chair subtly indicates the degree of authority it confers. As for the rest, every turn or carving of its members suggests an anecdote, real or fanciful, of people or events important in its time.

As might be expected, square and rigid was the chair of the Cromwell era. There was no graciousness nor grace in its stiff straight lines; no artistry in its sausage-like turnings. Its meagerness of luxury and comfort glaringly reflected the spartan spirit of the Puritans. Only an occasional piece of turkey-work in homemade or professional imitation of oriental carpets covered its low rectangular back and hard square seat, adding a touch of warmth and color to its uncompromising frame.

With the turn of a lathe, newly improved with a "key frame" attachment, the fat sausage-turnings of the Cromwellian chair were given a crisp, lively, spiral twist that changed the whole concept of the old rigid pattern at about the same time England's political pattern also changed. The ingenious new device was in effect a poppet, or lathe-head, containing a row of six or eight wooden wedges or "keys" firmly implanted through a horizontal, at intervals calculated to shape the required twist. These controlled the rotation of a shaft, each quarter turn or so of which sufficiently shifted off axis the revolving rod of wood being worked on, to gouge out the diagonal screw-like trough of a spiral turning. "Portuguese twist" they called it, for in Catherine's homeland the design had been popular so long that its origin in the spiral turnings of the East Indies was practically forgotten.

Cane, too, native to the Malay Peninsula, China, India, and Ceylon, was taken for granted in Portugal, where for decades it had been in-

28) Cromwellian chair, covered with original "turkey work." English, c. 1660. Governor's Office, Palace, Colonial Williamsburg.

29) Lathes of the 18th century. The lower one is an ancient pole lathe, the upper the later treadle or mandrel lathe, either one of which could be supplemented with a "key frame" for spiral turning. From John Barrow's *Supplement to the New & Universal Dictionary of Arts and Sciences*, 1754.

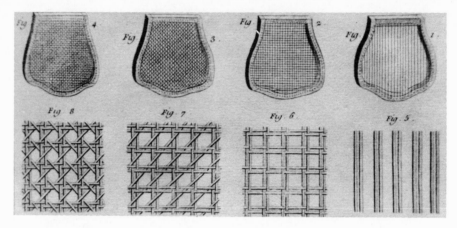

30) Four steps in caning. From Diderot's *Encyclopédie* (Paris, 1762–77), in which the figures were printed in reverse order.

cluded in cargoes from the Indies. Called "cane" when dried and yellow in color, it was a rattan that still showed distinct rings where sheathing leaves had been torn from its stem. Barely an inch in diameter, it was actually a kind of trailing palm that grew to the enormous length of five to six hundred feet, as it crept and hooked itself over tropical trees and bushes.

When bundles of cane began to appear in England in the strange and miscellaneous cargoes of the reactivated East India Company, a new trade was born, and a new fashion. Traditionally, chairs were made by housewrights or joiners. He who built a house also made everything that went into it. Chairs were "joyned" in the same way as a chest— heavy, straight, and four-square with only a pad or cushion for doubtful comfort. Gradually, here and there, now appeared a craftsman of the new trade, one who exclusively made chairs—cane chairs in the new fashion.

Built on the lines of the Cromwell chair, but with a spiral-twist frame, these new chairs usually were of "french Wallnuttree"; their seats and slightly concave, square backs of cane, woven of narrow strips in a wide, coarse mesh. Comfortable, strong, yet light enough to be easily moved about, cane chairs were an innovation; and in every home in England that wanted to forget the pinch of Puritan austerity, they were an immediate success. In London especially, they were bought by the dozen—for households which had been forced to burn their contents after an attack of the Plague of 1664, and those completely destroyed in the Great Fire that followed in its wake. And finally, the lucky ones, expanding in the glow of prosperity which now replaced years of adversity, bought cane chairs to be fashionable—for their halls, their bedrooms, and for sitting around the new gateleg tables, eating, drinking, playing basset, and generally gaming.

In his years of exile in the courts of Europe, Charles probably had never been told the Puritans' opinion, that dice were made of the bones of witches, and cards were cut from their skin. But if he had, he undoubtedly would have laid a wager that it wasn't so. For bets were made on the slightest excuse; and cards and dice had become a way of life in the highest circles of the land.

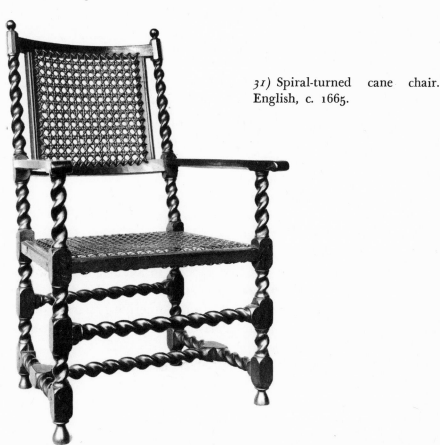

31) Spiral-turned cane chair. English, c. 1665.

32) One of a pair of matching Restoration side chairs of cane and beechwood with the "Boyes and Crowne" motif in stretcher and cresting. English, c. 1670.

Basset, played in Venice by ladies and gentlemen masked to avoid recognition, was a favorite form of gambling during the English Restoration. Evelyn describes one night at Court when "about twenty of the great courtiers and other dissolute people [played] at Basset round a large table, a bank of at least 2000 in gold before them."[4] The point of the insidious game was to outguess the others as to the order in which the cards would turn up. Not only gentlemen, but ladies too, "played deep," as the saying was. Pepys was told "that my Lady Castlemaine [Charles's most persistent mistress] is so great a gamester as to have won 15,000£ in one night and lost 25,000£ in another night, at play, and hath played 1000£ and 1500£ at a cast."[5] But neither Charles nor Catherine played for high stakes. In fact, Catherine preferred ombre, an intimate card game for three players, which she had learned in Portugal in her youth.

To accommodate all this table activity, the simple cane chair was soon elaborated. Its back grew narrow and taller, a cresting was added, and frequently—when intended for a wealthy customer—its spiral-twisted parts were "carved rich" and were "carved handsome." For ardent Royalists devoted to their King, Stuart roses cut into cresting and front stretchers were jostled by two deeply sculptured naked cherubs who held a crown between them, as if plucked right down from heaven. Casually referred to as "Boyes and Crowne" in the contemporary vernacular of Restoration carvers, only the thickly curled wigs worn by gentlemen of the period allowed noble heads to rest with any degree of comfort against this traditional symbol of the "Divine Right of Kings."

Wigs were a new conceit in England, at first affected by those who followed the French mode. Samuel Pepys decided on one the day he resolved "of putting me into a better garbe," beginning with "a good

33) "Five Orders of Perriwigs." Hogarth's ridicule of the vaunted importance of the wig as a badge of rank and position, as well as of the personalities who wore them, including Queen Charlotte and her ladies in waiting on the bottom row. A print after William Hogarth, 1761.

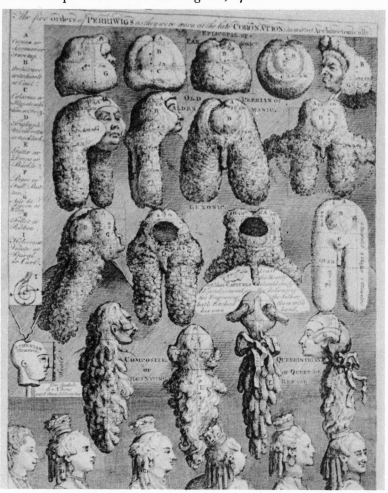

velvet cloak—that is, of cloth, lined with velvet, and other things modish, and a perruque."[6]

That was in October, 1663, while Catherine, the Queen, lay so desperately ill of spotted fever—"as full of the spots as a leopard"— that the next day Pepys temporarily "sent to stop the making of my velvet cloak, till I see whether she lives or dies." The talk around London was that "the King do seem to take it much to heart, for that he hath wept before her."[7] At Whitehall a week later, while walking in the long "Matted Gallery," Pepys suddenly "observed that the King is mighty gray," and he overheard the Duke of York say "that he was going to wear a perriwig; and they say the King also will."[8] By the tenth of November, he reported that the Queen "is now very well again, and that she hath bespoke herself a new gown."

Edmund Waller, the poet of the moment, credited Charles with the cure, as he rhymed:

> . . . *when no healing art prevail'd,*
> *When cordials and elixirs fail'd,*
> *On your pale cheek he dropt the shower,*
> *Reviv'd you like a dying flower.*[9]

As for the King, Pepys first saw Charles in a wig riding in Hyde Park the middle of the following April. It was a long, curly chestnut wig, for gray hair was not yet the fashion.

For those of simpler tastes, with wigs or without, Restoration chairs curved high into a so-called "Portuguese arch" or crown, and the front stretcher arched equally high to match or was turned into a large knob or two in the center, called a "Portuguese bulb." On some, the legs were also bulb-turned and ended in a "Braganza toe"—a channeled, tightly scrolled foot, slightly squared as if standing on turned-under knuckles. In Catherine's homeland, this is called a *pé de pincel*—a paint-brush foot.

To those unacquainted with Catherine, the channeled scroll foot is "Spanish," and a leg of elongated C-scrolls is called a "Flemish" scroll. In fact, to some, the English Restoration chair, no matter what its parts, is categorically "Spanish." In Spain, however, its national counterpart is still called "Portuguese."

When not made of "french Wallnuttree," chairs were painted black

34) Portuguese side chair, late 17th century. Back and seat of embossed leather edged with large brass studs, the posts topped by delicate brass finials. The interlocked scrolls of the front stretcher combine to make a "Portuguese" arch, while the rear stretcher is turned into a rudimentary double "Portuguese" bulb. In Portugal the so-called "Spanish" foot is called a *pé de pincel,* or paint-brush foot.

to simulate the expensive ebony Catherine had made the fashion. Or they were lacquered red or green or black, and crowded with little painted figures of synthetic Chinamen. The combination of foreign cultures and strange techniques that is the Restoration chair, only hints at how the diverse wealth of Catherine's dowry touched every trade and home in England.

Wool weavers were especially affected. For at the same time that

35) English chair of beech, japanned in green and gold in imitation of oriental lacquer and caned extremely fine. C. 1720. One of a set of six made in London for the export market.

calico first became a menace to them, they were also threatened by the new vogue for cane as it was ever more frequently stretched and tightly woven across the backs and seats of the tall, narrow chairs of the period. As the popularity of cane chairs increased—and they were made by the thousands for home consumption and for export—wool weavers all over England felt the pinch of fashion. Frantically they petitioned Parliament in 1680 to suppress the manufacture of cane chairs. For they claimed that the increased use of cane caused not only the loss of appreciable yardage in the original upholstery of chairs but also the very lucrative repeat business the wool weavers had come to expect from the inevitable damage of moths.

The petition was denied. The wool interests, who in the inherited memory of every Englishman had always held paramount place in the English economy, were now having their traditional advantage usurped by those upstarts connected with the newly flourishing East India trade. The wail of the wool weaver was to continue for a hundred years, but those of the generation living during the last quarter of the seventeenth century were the first to be seriously affected by the influx of exotic trade goods. They could still remember the "old days" and wished them back.

They remembered, according to a popular broadside of the time,

> *When first the India trade began,*
> *And ships beyond the tropics ran*
> *In quest of various drugs and spices,*
> *And sundry other strange devices, . . .*

East India ships did not then

> *. . . carry gold or bullion*
> *To fetch home what supplants our woollen;*
> *Nor were this nation fond to wear*
> *Such Indian toys which cost so dear . . .*

Those were the days when

> *This nation then was rich and wealthy*
> *And in a state which we call'd healthy. . . .*

But, continued the doggerel, the India trade

> *. . . was drove on by such measures*
> *As soon exhausted much our treasures;*
> *For then our chiefest artists went*
> *With patterns, and with money sent,*
> *To make and purchase Indian ware,*
> *For which this Nation pays full dear. . . .*

To the grief of the workers of England, these exotic imports, encouraged

> *. . . by lords and ladies, dukes and duchess,*
> *So far prevailed as set the fashion*
> *Which, plague-like, soon spread o'er the nation.*
> *Our ladies all were set a gadding,*

After these toys they ran a madding;
And nothing then would please their fancies,
Nor Dolls, nor Joans, nor wanton Nancies
Unless it was of Indian's making;
And if 'twas so, 'twas wondrous taking. . . .

Despite petitions to Parliament, and broadsides such as this, written to arouse public opinion,

This antick humour so prevailed,
Tho' many 'gainst it greatly railed,
'Mongst all degrees of female kind
That nothing else could please their mind. . . .[10]

And nothing else did for a good fifty years. Styles, of course, would change, but always the special difference of "Indian ware"—anything from the East—was considered "high fashion."

As for cane, that stayed in favor until after the turn of the century. But not only for chairs, for daybeds too, new to this era of fashionable lounging, with backs that echoed chair-back designs. And stools for sitting were made of cane, even tabletops were woven of the foreign stuff. Charles II also had a screen of cane, not to shield him from a draft, but specifically "to preserve the Bedde from being spoyled by the Doggs."[11] His were special dogs, tiny, intelligent, black and white spaniels on dapper legs, that to this day are known as "King Charles Spaniels." They well deserve the name, for according to Evelyn, the King adored his spaniels, which "follow him and lie in his bed-chamber, where he often suffered the bitches to puppy and give suck, which rendered it very offensive, and indeed made the whole court nasty and stinking."[12] The dogs apparently had found a way around the screen and, in the manner of their kind, also into the heart of the King.

Too many, humans particularly, found their way into the heart of the King, and for greater profit, into his pocket. By August 1667, the royal purse was empty again. All usual sources of revenue and credit were exhausted. Even the King's personal laundry was down to "no hankerchers and but three bands to his neck"[13]—the linen draper being owed £5000. Pepys writes that on the 24th "comes a letter . . . to invite us,

36) Cane reading stand on a cane-top table with a banister-back chair of
Charles II's time. English, c. 1675–80.

which is as much as to fright us, into lending the King money . . ."[14]

Years later, it was not in money that Pepys's Navy associate and
neighbor, Admiral Sir William Penn, was repaid for his loan. To the
satisfaction of all concerned, it was in land—a large slice of North
America, dubbed "Pensilvania" or Penn's Wood. For Charles II, that

Come all ye Saints that would for little Buy ,
Great Tracts of Land, and care not where they lye ,
Deal with your Quaking Friends, they're Men of Light,
The Spirit hates Deceit and Scorns to Bite . ——

37) Playing card used to adver-
tise William Penn's "Holy Experiment."

was the cheapest way to discharge a debt in 1681; and for William Penn, the Admiral's son and heir, it was the richest fulfillment of a dream, ever.

To make Penn's dream a success, land companies ventured to sell his enthusiasm and his land where every flip of a card brought riches to someone. At basset tables throughout England, playing cards circulated by The Pennsylvania Company sold land, and possibly religion, to any who stopped long enough in their play to read the rhyming doggerels, different on each card.

> *Come all ye Saints that would for little Buy,*
> *Great Tracts of Land, and care not where they lye,*
> *Deal with your Quaking Friends, they're Men of Light,*
> *The Spirit hates Deceit and Scorns to Bite.*[15]

By the shipload they came—to Pennsylvania just as they continued to come to Massachusetts, Maryland, and Virginia. Even as today, families uprooted carry along their most precious possessions to a new homeland, so these Puritans, Quakers, and Cavaliers brought all the goods and chattels the little ships could hold. For four months or longer, while crossing the choppy Atlantic, pets and children crawled over chests of clothes, between bedding and cooking utensils, and under the tables and chairs that were to be the first furnishings in the new land.

In all the colonies, by the end of the seventeenth century, simple furniture was made locally whenever housewrights found time from the building of homes. But cane chairs were luxuries only to be had in Boston or Philadelphia, and then only when a merchant advertised some as "lately arrived from England." Wealthy citizens ordered directly from London, like Salem's Judge Sewall, who in 1720 sent for "a Duzen of good black Walnut Chairs, fine Cane, with a Couch" and for a second dozen "of a different figure."[16] At that time, cane chairs, called "India" chairs in the colonies, were also bought by the dozen with southern tobacco, and were landed at plantation wharves after no greater time lapse than it took to deliver an equal order from London overland to any estate in the English countryside.

As long as they were in fashion, "India" chairs continued to arrive

38) High-back cane chair from England that William Penn used in America.

from England, for the colonies had no direct way of acquiring cane, nor for that matter anything else from the East. But eventually a cane-chair maker found his way to Philadelphia with a supply of the supple stuff, for he advertised in the *Pennsylvania Gazette* on June 27, 1734, that "next to the Sign of the Pewter Platter in Front Street" he made "Cane Chairs of all Sorts . . . after the best & newest Fashion." His biggest business, though, was probably in the "old Chairs caned or

39) American walnut version of a low-back Cromwellian chair, with spiral spindles substituting for cane. The plank seat is slightly sunk to accommodate a thin cushion. New Jersey, late 17th century.

40) American "banister-back," early 18th century. The block and ball turnings of the front legs ending in a grooved "Spanish" foot echo the turnings of the Portuguese chair, as does the turned double-bulb front stretcher. Four split-spindles substitute for a back of woven cane, and rush for a cane seat.

41) American side chair of maple, with nail-studded leather instead of cane on seat and back, and "Spanish" front feet. **C.** 1700–1725.

Holes mended (if not gone too far),"[17] which he promised to do "at reasonable rates."

In the meantime, up and down the coast, wherever people caught a glimpse of the latest imports from England and the Continent, cane chairs were copied in simplified style. Three to five vertical split-spindles, flat side forward, substituted for backs of India cane, while local rush was woven into comfortable seats for the chairs we now call "banister-backs."

With conscientious skill early American ingenuity used local products to translate European fashions into local needs. Cultures as diversified as their ancestry have left traces more or less pronounced on every piece American craftsmen put their hands to. But through all the years that have elapsed since Catherine's dowry revitalized the English East India Company, it has been the East that in subtle little ways, as well as with wholly transplanted arts, has refined and polished domestic taste.

CHAPTER SIX

Precious Lacquer-ware

"The Queen brought over with her from Portugal such Indian cabinets as had never before been seen here."

— JOHN EVELYN, *June 9, 1662*

WHILE the public part of Catherine's dowry was attacked pro and con as to its national advantage, her personal appointments were being both loudly criticized and openly admired. After the first sharp comments at the outlandish appearance of Catherine and her Portuguese retinue, appraising eyes began privately to approve the "Indian cabinets" that studded her Hampton Court apartments like so many smoldering gems.

Cabinets were an important part of seventeenth-century decor, for it was an age that coveted and acquired mementoes of each glimpse into the wonders of the expanding world. Agates, onyxes, and intaglios; a lump of amber with a toad enclosed; the eggs of rare birds; or a skull carved of wood by Albrecht Dürer—such were the "curiosities" and "rarities" that composed the cabinet collection of every would-be "virtuoso." In fact, some of these talented gentlemen with inquisitive minds were quite inadvertently assembling in their cabinets the beginnings of several of today's oldest museums.

To house such treasures, cabinets of the finest workmanship were a matter of rivalry and pride. In all of England there were none more handsome than straight-sided so-called "Indian" cabinets, varying in size and vying in splendor. Behind single or double doors that fastened shut with a sliding bolt mounted on an elaborate, hand-wrought metal escutcheon, were concealed arrangements of niches and drawers, ideal for accumulations of Caesar medallions, miniatures by Peter Oliver (the current favorite), even for miscellaneous collections of shells and uncut precious stones.

Variously called "Chinese," "Japanese," or "Indian," they represented a vague, exotic, colorful, confused world to seventeenth-century Europeans. The confusion arose from the fact that a lacquer cabinet took on the name of the country, the district, or the port from which it was shipped. The choice was made by English taste and fashion, whether for "Bantam-work" or "Coromandel," for other Chinese lacquer or for the type the Japanese sold to no foreigner, except the Dutch or the Chinese.

The only accurate information about Chinese crafts and customs to reach Europe was in the voluminous letters such French Jesuit priests as Pères Louis Le Compte, Gaston Laurent Cœurdoux, and François Xavier d'Entrecolles sent back home to patrons and superiors. Le Compte's were published as *Memoirs* in 1696, while Cœurdoux's and d'Entrecolles's found their way into the *Lettres Edifiantes et Curieuses Ecrites des Missions Etrangères* of the Society of Jesus, beginning in 1702. Several decades later, Père Jean Baptiste du Halde, secretary of the Society in Paris, collected the correspondence of twenty-four years with these and other Jesuit missionaries from all over China into a fabulous *Description of the Empire of China,* which was promptly translated into English in 1738.

From du Halde we learn that according to legend, it was the Chinese who perfected lacquer before they even devised a means of recording time. Out of the sap of what he called the "Varnish-Tree"—Asian cousin to our poison ivy—they distilled "the Liquor [which] has certain venomous Qualities. However that be," he added, " 'tis certain this Varnish (or Japan) is not less esteem'd on that account."[1] The records bear him out, since for a thousand years before Christ, certain regions in China accepted lacquer-ware even in payment of taxes. Later in

42) Blue and white Chinese porcelain vase, showing a Chinese chair in the process of being lacquered. Ch'ien Lung (1736–95). The design is thought to have been copied from a Ming dynasty painting.

Japan, where Buddhist monks carried the secret around A.D. 500, things covered with lacquer were also valued precious enough for the treasury.

By the mid-seventeenth century, by the time the Manchus had displaced the Ming dynasty, lacquer was "much in use amongst" the Chinese. So wrote John Nieuhoff, steward to the embassy of the Dutch East India Company that in 1644 made unsuccessful overtures to the new regime at Peking. He noticed the Chinese used lacquer to "colour or paint their Household-stuff, Ships, and Houses, that they make them shine and glister like Looking-glasses." Except in palaces, though, rarely more than an occasional piece of furniture in any one room was lacquered, and that to give an accent of contrast in texture and color to the traditional highly polished dark woods. But when a table was lacquered, the Chinese according to Nieuhoff "use no Tablecloths at their Meals; for if they spill any grease or other liquor upon the Table, it is easily rubbed off with a little fair water, without loss or damage of colour."[2]

To western eyes, however, it was the glow—the subdued sheen of finely polished lacquer—that gave it its value; it was the glimpse into a strangely exotic world spread across its surface, that clothed each piece in enchanted beauty. Few, though, were those Europeans who saw in its satin smoothness the days stretching into weeks of knowing application, of endless polishing, or who even guessed there was symbolism in the decoration.

Starting with a board of soft, even-grained pine, Chinese artisans primed the wood with a film of sticky lacquer, then pressed on hempen cloth to form a base. Twelve to twenty-four hours later, the piece was hard enough to be polished smooth with whetstone, and another coat of lacquer was added. Twenty, thirty, or more applications were each carefully brushed or flowed on—not too slowly lest the lacquer dry too hard, nor too quickly for then it would be neither smooth nor hard enough, but with just the speed learned by experience. Twenty, thirty, or more times the piece rested for one, sometimes three days, in the moist atmosphere of a special cave or chamber, for only in dampness can lacquer properly mature, and in a damp climate survive. When sufficiently hardened, each layer, just as if it were the last, was "water-planed" to a reflection with felt or leather, or simply by the nimble gliding fingers of practiced workmen.

Not all, but much of the lacquer-ware they worked on was black, a deep bottomless black, on which native artists recorded in color and gold the scenes around them, or pictured the legends they loved and lived with. However, when lacquer was in color, it was warm buff or brown; a deep green called olive; or *aubergine*—the rich, coppery plum color of an eggplant. Then of course, there was red—red lacquer—like no other red in the world, for it was colored with cinnabar, red sulphuret of mercury, the native vermilion.

Halfway around the globe, where spreading wealth fostered luxury and extravagance, lacquer cabinets became the passion of the West, no matter what the color. Collectors of "rarities" collected cabinets as well. The Portuguese Ambassador stationed at the Court of St. James's while Catherine was Queen owned at least a dozen, according to John Evelyn.[3] The craze for as many lacquer cabinets as the purse could buy spread well beyond court circles—for walnut, the fashionable wood of the Continent, was scarce in England, and the handsome richness of lacquer fitted the mania for ostentation that possessed the Restoration.

Rich they were and handsome, yet in size and shape each cabinet conformed to custom as practiced in its country of origin. Low ones on short dumpy legs came from Japan, where all furniture was low for the convenience of a people who preferred to kneel upon the floor rather than to sit on chairs—a custom acquired from the Chinese at about the same time the secrets of lacquering passed from China to Japan. Long before the seventeenth century, however, the chair was in common use in China, and other furniture had been raised accordingly, all except those pieces customarily used upon the *k'ang*, the elevated brick sleeping platform still used in Chinese homes, which is heated from beneath against China's colder climate. Otherwise, cabinets from China were usually chest-on-chests behind two pairs of double doors, the combination as much as eight to ten feet tall. Yet when they reached England, double chests were often separated, each half placed upon the same kind of ornate stand that raised low Japanese cabinets off English floors. East met West in ill-assorted combination each time a jewel of a lacquer cabinet was dramatically set upon an English stand,

43) Black and gold Chinese lacquer cabinet crowned by a cresting and raised on a stand of English carved and gilded pinewood. Late 17th century.

grossly carved with dragon-scaled baroque scrolls wound round the "Boyes and Crowne" of the Restoration. For added elegance, many cabinets were even topped with a cornice to match the stand, both carved of lime or pear wood, and, in the fashion of the times, covered with silver or silver gilt. By the first quarter of the eighteenth century, tastes were simpler, cornices disappeared, and English-made stands turned Chinese in feeling—some, in fact, were actually made in China.

However, when Catherine was Queen, the East was still a year away from England. The thirteen, or even eighteen, ships sent out during a season could not begin to carry back enough lacquer cabinets to satisfy the unrestrained rivalry for fabulous possessions that spiraled like inflation through England. By way of compensation, buried in the "wealth of confusion" of murky holds, which reeked a medley of spicy Eastern odors, and jammed up against the few bulky cabinets that crowded the limited space, were stacks of lacquer screens. Eight, ten, as many as twelve leaves folded one upon the other into piles of concentrated eastern artistry.

Tall, standing screens were indispensable furniture in the East. On them native craftsmen lavished the accumulated skill of ten lifetimes. Son, like father, like grandfather, followed tradition in picturing a story across the polished lacquer surface of one leaf after another, in the particular technique of his neighborhood and generation.

Since the Sung dynasty (A.D. 960–1280), some Chinese lacquer-ware had been "incrusted" with figures clothed in bits of mother-of-pearl, soapstone, or jade, hands and faces flatly carved from ivory; and the shimmer of water suggested by leaves of crinkled lead or tin. "Men, Mountains, Palaces, Huntings, Birds, Combats and several Figures,"[4] was the way Louis Le Compte, the traveling Jesuit missionary, described these tantalizing glimpses into a colorful never-never land.

By the seventeenth century, with the increase of the export trade, the technique changed. Instead of using hard stones, figures now were modeled within drawn outlines, built up with a putty made of powdered charcoal, white lead, lampblack, and camphor mixed with lacquer. Then with tiny chisels less than a quarter inch across, they were cut and scraped and carved into hills and gulleys, lines and folds, accents and expressions, in which "point the *Chineses* are Magnificent for small Charges."[5]

Or, in reverse of this technique, thirty or more layers of different-colored lacquers were built up in a carefully planned arrangement to be carved intaglio. Within the outlines of landscapes with pavilions, children at play, assortments of instruments used in the arts and sciences and called the "Hundred Antiques," as well as an occasional dragon, phoenix, *ch'i-lin* or *kylin,* or a long-tailed tortoise, the tiny wedge-shaped graver sliced down to the exact layer of color required. Held by a steady hand, now deep, now shallow would it cut, baring without mishap the green, the red, the *aubergine* against the polished black expanse of screen or cabinet.

This "engraved" lacquer was dubbed "Bantam-work" from the time that the first Dutch traders shipped some home from Bantam in Java. Not until the English East India Company had long been established on the Coromandel Coast of India did the same lacquer-work sent from there gradually take on the name "Coromandel." "Bantam" and "Coromandel" were only the names of spots touched by East India ships. Chinese lacquer-ware actually was made around Peking or Soochow, in Tongking, Nanking, and in Cochin China.

As to the meaning of Chinese designs—they spoke a secret language which has been much garbled by time and distance. For the initiated, they are filled with the symbolism of no less than three religions, with the attributes and emblems of rank, and with a constant pictorial play upon words. But the lacquer-ware which probably excited western curiosity the most was that which showed people at work at their trades or a glimpse into Chinese high society.

It was "out of old Skreens"—"India" screens—that new cabinets were made in England, "by the help of a Joyner." According to John Stalker, who published a *Treatise of Japanning and Varnishing* in 1688, joiners "never [did] consider the situation of their figures; so that in these things so torn and hacked to joint a new fancie, you may observe the finest hodgpodg and medley of Men and Trees turned topsie turvie. . . ." After listing several incongruities, he summarized, "In a word, they have so mixed and blended the Elements together, have made a league between fire and water, and have forc't the clouds and mountains to shake hands, nay deprived every thing of its due site and position, that if it were like any thing, beside ruin and deformity, it must represent to you the Earth, when Noah's Flood was overwhelming it."[6]

Not so the "contrivances of Japan screens [used] instead of wainscot" that in 1682 John Evelyn admired in the home of a neighbor, one

44) An English looking-glass frame, "hacked to joint a new fancie." Covered with incised lacquer probably cut from a Chinese screen and applied with no regard for the design; the top and bottom pieces even put on crosswise. C. 1675.

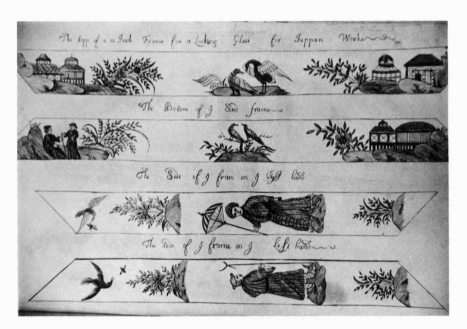

45) Stalker's designs for a looking-glass frame of "Jappan Worke." From John Stalker's *Treatise of Japanning and Varnishing*, 1688.

"whose whole house is a cabinet of all elegancies, especially Indian."
Mixing his geography in the vernacular of the times, Evelyn added that
the "landscapes" of the screens were panoramically drawn to "represent
the manner of living, and country of the Chinese."[7] Or so he thought,
for probably not ten people in England, besides those manning East
India ships, had ever seen a native Chinese. As for traveling through
that country, the "landscapes" on screens were likely to be as true an
account of the interior as many written ones, for, according to du Halde,
"a great many [were] trifling and false Relations . . . a Parcel of Absurdities and Lyes."[8] Yet from screens just like these, generations of
English craftsmen were to copy their designs for everything from pottery
to wallpaper. Eventually the Chinese even copied English copies of
their early work, to satisfy the insatiable demand for things "in the
Chinese Taste."

By 1697, the East India Company had become so sensitive to the
demands at home that one order alone in their letter book of that
year lists: "60 cabinets, viz. 20 of the black ground, inlayed with mother-
of-pearl with figures, 10 black & gold, 20 of engraved work, the ground
gold, with Landscapes and figures. 20 sets of screens, 12 leaves of a set,
8, 9 & 10 feet high by 20 to 24 inches broad; black & gold, with Landscapes & figures engraved on a gold ground."[9] Following this were
seven items of various sorts of carefully described lacquer tables adding
up to the unbelievable number of one thousand nine hundred and
twenty! Three years later, the Joiners' Company petitioned against
the importation of furniture from the East Indies.

Probably the lacquer-ware in Catherine's personal dowry, more than
any other of her possessions, first brought forcibly home to England
the fantastic wealth inherent in her public dowry gift of Bombay. The
East India Company was certainly aware of an unprecedented resurgence of trade after the transfer to them of that key port.

Not all lacquer-ware, however, was imported by the Company. As
early as May 23, 1663, barely a year after all of London had been agog
over Catherine's spectacular "Indian" cabinets, Pepys paid a visit to
a man by the name of "Greatorex" who had invented a domestic varnish
that to Pepys "appear[ed] every whit as good, upon a stick which he
hath done, as the Indian."[10] Greatorex was probably only one of many
who attempted to capitalize on the current vogue.

46) Designs for a cabinet, "to be Placed according to yoʳ fancy." From John Stalker's *Treatise of Japanning and Varnishing*, 1688.

47) Japanned hanging corner cupboard, decorated with an English version of a Chinese leading a spotted deer through an imaginary landscape. English, c. 1715.

48) Twelve-scallop, tilt-top, English tea table, japanned in black and gold. C. 1750. Palace Parlor, Colonial Williamsburg.

But it was John Stalker's *Treatise . . . , Being a Compleat Discovery of Those Arts*—from the English point of view—that popularized "japanning" for the amateur. The book went through several editions at the astounding price of £75 a copy. Hardly had its third edition been published in 1689, than eight-year-old Mary Verney of "Claydon" was given her father's permission "to learn to Jappan, as you call it, . . . therefore learn in God's name all Good Things, and I will willingly be at the Charge so farr as I am able—tho They come from never so farr and Looke of an Indian Hue and Odour, . . ."[11]

So rapidly had this new "art" intrigued the public that by 1710

London's professional japanners were numerous enough to petition Parliament to prohibit "merchants sending over English patterns and models to India, and buying such quantities of India lacquered wares." They declared that "the curious and ingenious art and mystery of japanning, so much improved in England of late years [had been brought] to so great perfection as to exceed all manner of Indian lacquer, and to equal the right japan itself, . . ."[12]

All kinds of Chinese lacquers were generically spoken of as "Indian," meaning of course East Indian; while "right japan" was lacquer-ware from Japan. As for the difference between the two, Stalker explains that "the Japan-Artist works most of all in Gold, and other metals; the Bantam for the generality in Colours, with a very small sprinkling of Gold here and there, like the patches in a Ladies countenance."[13] The Japanese were actually more meticulous in their workmanship, but lacked the charm of the free artistry of Chinese design.

Even though since 1624 only the Dutch and the Chinese had been permitted to trade directly with Japan, the English East India Company picked up what Japanese things they could at Bantam, Taiwan, and the free port of Amoy. The very inaccessibility of Japan gave it the added glamour of the unknown, and actually added words to the English language. A black varnished walking cane was called a "japan" in 1678, and in 1680 the Earl of Rochester rhymed in his published *Poems:*

> *Kiss me thou curious picture of a man;*
> *How odd thou art, how pretty, how japan!*[14]

But it was Stalker who first coined the word "japanning," which was applied to all occidental attempts at a truly oriental art. In fact, Stalker contended in his *Treatise* in 1688 that Chinese lacquers were "almost obsolete, and out of fashion, out of use, and neglected." He proposed that by "means [of his instruction book] the Nobility & Gentry might be compleatly furnisht with whole Setts of Japan-work . . . [and not be] forced to content themselves with . . . some odd thing that had not a fellow to answer it." But he warned against "all the cheats and cousenage of those whiffling, impotent fellows, who pretend to teach young Ladies that Art."[15]

There must have been many such, for, as Mrs. Delany put it in 1727,

Cloth
Brushes

Combs
Brushes

A Pincushing Truncke for Pendents Necklace Rings & Jewells

49) Designs for brushes and "a Pincushing Truncke for Pendents Necklace Rings & Jewells." From John Stalker's *Treatise of Japanning and Varnishing*, 1688.

50) An American japanned high chest-of-drawers, each drawer marked with "Pim" in chalk, which leads to the conclusion that the chest was made by John Pimm, a cabinetmaker of Boston, active 1732–67. It was japanned by an unknown artisan and its sides painted to simulate tortoise-shell. Not one of its exotic embellishments is to be found in Stalker's *Treatise*. C. 1740–50. Readbourne Parlor, The Henry Francis duPont Winterthur Museum.

"everybody's mad about Japan work."[16] She had reason to know, for even though she was "genteel" poor, she moved in court circles, was a friend of Handel and Swift, and left volumes of letters to prove it. As many of her kind, she was adept at every sort of handwork she ever heard of, yet she claimed to be only "a dab" at japanning. But Lady Walpole had become so proficient that the *New & Curious Method of Japanning* manual was dedicated to her.

The varnish these dilettantes used was of domestic vintage, of some animal or vegetable secretion such as seed-lac, dragon's blood, or isinglass, which had none of the anti-social characteristics of *Rhus vernicifera,* the Chinese "Varnish Tree." And those who imitated the raised "Indian" lacquer, substituted putty, gesso, compo, whatever they had, for the foreign ingredients, and touched the figures with yellow if they lacked gold.

Japanning was even practiced in the colonies, for London fashions sailed across the Atlantic as fast as the wind could blow them there. In Boston, a little less Puritan by 1713, "Nehemiah Partridge Japanner upon the Mill Bridge" advertised his "reasonable Rates" on September 21.[17] He was probably the second japanner there, for Samuel Sewall had witnessed the accident which cost the life of "Pendleton, the Japanner," more than a year before.[18] By 1732, one Thomas Johnson was a sufficiently sophisticated artisan to have a trade card engraved "Japanner at the Golden Lyon in Ann Street Boston";[19] and John Waghorne, who had taught japanning to "several Ladies of the first Quality in England," advertised in 1739 that he would instruct Boston "Ladies to Japan in the newest Method invented for the Purpose, which exceeds all other Japanning for Beauty."[20] New Yorkers, long supplied through the Dutch West India Company, apparently were slower to simulate "right japan," or the records have been misplaced. Not until January 6, 1735, did "Gerardus Duyckinck at the Sign of the two Cupids, near the Old Slip Market" inform his neighbors that he made and had for sale "looking-glasses new Silvered, and the Frames plaine Japan'd or Flowered."[21]

In London by that date, this "art and mystery" of the East had temporarily gone out of fashion. With the resurgence of the "Chinese Taste" in the 1750s, however, it was again in high favor, but from a completely western point of view. Du Halde had written that lacquering was one of those "Kinds of Arts that are necessary for the common Uses of Life," at which the Chinese labored "with a certain kind of Elegance agreeable to their Taste."[22] Yet no seventeenth-century Englishman had a hint that within one generation after these jewel-like pieces arrived in Catherine's dowry lacquer would be an established part of the English decorative idiom.

CHAPTER SEVEN

Tea Economics

 "On Tea commended by Her Majesty"

— E D M U N D   W A L L E R

W HEN Catherine was Queen, festivities at the English court began on St. Catherine's Day, the Queen's birthday, and continued from November twenty-fifth through the foul weather months
of an English winter until Charles's birthday on the twenty-ninth of
May. Gradually, Catherine began to drop her youthful Portuguese
inhibitions, and ever more frequently joined in the flagrantly gay and
boisterous activities of her adopted home. She even spoke "now very
pretty English"[1] according to Pepys, and by the end of 1663 often coined
quaintly alien phrases to the amusement of her hearers.

She also had learned to dance to please Charles, and to the delight of
her royal husband, found that she actually loved it. "My wife hath given
a good introduction to such a business," Charles wrote his sister in Paris,
"for the other day she made . . . her chaplins dance country dances in her
bed chamber."[2] By the time of her Birthday Ball the year she was twenty-
eight, she was ready to take Charles's hand before the assembled élite of
England and be led to join fourteen other couples in the branle, or
brawl, a popular group dance in which kissing was part of the routine.
Pepys had come early that night to view the spectacle, "and with much

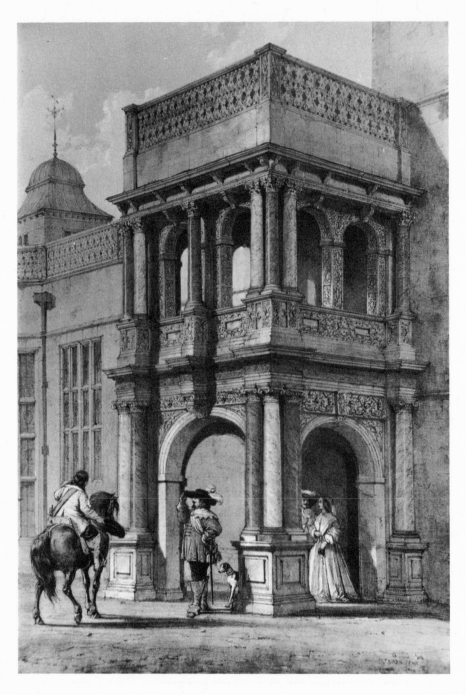

51) Porch at "Audley End," Essex. From *The Mansions of England in the Olden Times,* Joseph Nash, 1840.

ado got up to the loft, where with much trouble I could see very well. Anon the house grew full, and the candles light, and the King and Queen and all the ladies sat . . . all most excellently dressed in rich petticoats and gowns, and dyamonds, and pearls."[3]

A few years later, when "frolics" were a bored court's entertainment, Catherine even joined masked courtiers in hackney chairs on their rounds of crashing private parties incognito. Charles had actually urged her when she had been hardly eight months at the Court of St. James's, "to follow Q-mother of France's example and goe in masquerade before the carnavall be done."[4] As a matter of fact, it took her five years to enter into the spirit of the "extravagances" of masquerading, but when she did, she did it with gusto.

Her escapade at the annual fair of Saffron Walden while the court was at Audley End in October 1670 is notorious. It seems that she together with the Duchess of Richmond and the Duchess of Buckingham, each riding pinion behind an obliging gentleman—Catherine on a "cart jade"—"had a frolick to disguise themselves like country lasses, in red petticoats, wastcotes, etc., and so goe see the faire." According to the witness, "They had all so overdone it in their disguise, and looked so much more like antiques than country volk," that they were immediately followed by the inquisitive natives, right into the booth where Catherine went "to buy a pair of yellow stockings for her sweet hart," her escort "asking for a pair of gloves sticht with blew, for his sweet hart." The masqueraders were found to be strangers "by their gebrish,"[5] and Catherine was recognized as the Queen, a combination of circumstances which sent the frolickers fleeing on their nags, followed by the motley crowd, right up to the court gate of Audley End.

But in her quieter moments, Catherine loved a picnic, when her ladies "treated her by everyone bringing their dish, who then attended her into the forest, and she eat under a tree . . . The Queen was wonderfully pleased and merry, . . ."[6] She had been much concerned at first "that English ladies spend so much time in dressing themselves" that she feared they had little left for "God Almighty, and . . . housewifery."[7] Yet while Catherine practiced their English ways with a Portuguese accent, English ladies learned enough Portuguese "housewifery" from Catherine to brew a cup of tea solely for pleasure.

No Englishman at that time considered tea drinking a pleasure. In fact, barely four years before Catherine came to England, tea had been

introduced as a medicine: "That excellent and by all Physitians approved China Drink called by the Chineans *Tcha,* by other nations
Tay, alias Tee."[8] In 1660, Thomas Garway, the first English dealer in
tea, hailed it as the panacea for "preserving a perfect health until extreme Old Age," and listed the nagging afflictions that tea could
alleviate.

> It maketh the Body active and lusty.
> It helpeth the Headache giddiness and heaviness thereof.
> It vanquisheth heavy Dreams, easeth the Brain, and strengtheneth the
>   Memory.
> It is good against Lipitude Distillations, and cleareth the Sight.
> It is good against Crudities, strengthening the weakness of the Ventri-
>   cle or Stomach, causing good Appetite and Digestion, and particu-
>   larly for Men of a corpulent Body, and such as are great eaters of
>   Flesh.
> It prevents and cures Agues, Surfets and Fevers, . . .
> It is good for Colds, Dropsies and Scurveys, if properly infused, . . .
>   and expelleth Infection.[9] [Et cetera, et cetera, et cetera.]

These, though, were not the reasons for drinking tea in Catherine's
native Portugal. There tea had been known since the earliest trading

52) Japanese hostess about to
make a bowl of tea for *cha-no-
yu.*

carracks had sailed home with their creaking hulls crammed with the strange and exciting products of the East. Naked Chinese feet had stamped tea for export into square wooden boxes, lined with thin lead; and deft yellow hands had packed in straw the pots and tiny Chinese bowls of hard-fired red earth the Portuguese called *búcaro*.* Finer than the best pottery made in the West, this curious Chinese teaware, "red porcelain" to the English, changed tea drinking from a cure into a pleasure. Together, tea and porcelain upset the established pattern of western living.

According to the Chinese, the origins of tea are shrouded in legend. In the year A.D. 543, a missionary called Bodhidharma came out of India to meditate for nine sleepless years on the virtues of Buddha. After only three, he fell asleep. To prevent another lapse of consciousness, he cut off his eyelids and threw them on the ground beside him. When he again felt drowsy, he munched some leaves from the shrub that had grown on the spot, and was refreshed. The shrub, they say, was the tea plant, *Camellia Thea.*

Some twelve centuries later, Ch'ien Lung described the brewing of tea and the transcendent pleasures of drinking the brew in an "Ode Upon Tea," the musical singsong of which creeps into even this fragment of translation:

> . . . *put upon a moderate fire a three-legged vase*
> *of which the colour and the form indicate its long service;*
>   *fill it with clean water of melted snow;*
>   *heat the water to the degree necessary*
>   *to blanch the fish or redden the crab;*
>   *pour it in a cup made of the earth of Yué;*
> *upon the tender leaves of a choice tree leave it in repose*
> *until the vapours which first rise in abundance form thick clouds;*
>   *then gradually disperse until there is*
>   *only a light fog upon the surface;*
> *then quaff without precipitation this delicious liquor; . . .*

* *A word of Spanish origin, applied both to the clay and to the vessels made of it. According to the* Diccionario de la Real Academia Española, *the clay is "found in various parts of the world . . . It has a pleasant odor particularly when . . . wet, and women used to chew it and even eat it . . ."*

*One may taste, one may feel but one is never able to express
the sweet tranquillity imported by a beverage so prepared . . .*[10]

Time and custom in the East have irrevocably interwoven tea with
religious meditation, but in Japan since the sixteenth century, ceremonial tea drinking has included the reverent contemplation of beauty.
There in simple, dedicated tearooms, the art of *cha-no-yu,* the tea ceremony, is still performed according to the exacting rules prescribed four
hundred years ago. Languid grace and conscious serenity govern every
studied movement of the participants, and a rigid formula even dictates
conversation. Centuries of ceremonial tea drinking in the East have
enveloped humble, homely duties with dignity and beauty and have
bred a bland civility into a continent.

But the average, matter-of-fact Restoration Englishman had no such
understanding of tea; his drink was beer, ale, or cider, with occasionally
"a good sack posset" made of hot milk curdled by ale or a wine such as

53) An artist's two plans for a formal Japanese teahouse and garden. From
Tsukiyama Teizō-den, an old Japanese text on landscape gardening.

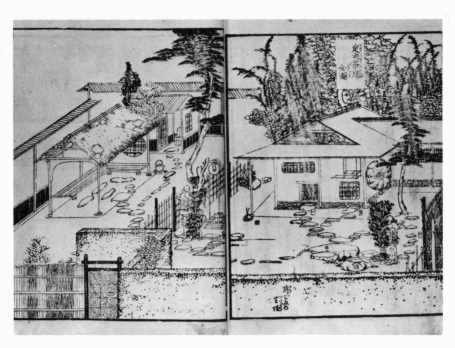

sack, sweetened, spiced, and thickened with bread sops. In coffeehouses, new to London in 1652, tea was first sold by the cup or "dish" full, and was taxed 8d. a gallon. It may have been to "Garraway's," Tom Garway's famous coffeehouse, that Samuel Pepys "did send for a cup of tea, (a China drink) of which I never had drank before."[11] That was in 1660, the same year Garway recommended tea as a nostrum for his long roster of nasty complaints. Only once again, seven years later, did Pepys mention the beverage. "Home, and there find my wife making of tea; a drink which Mr. Pelling, the Potticary, tells her is good for her cold and defluxions."[12]

At Whitehall in the meantime, the poet Edmund Waller wrote an ode, "On Tea commended by Her Majesty," in compliment to Catherine on her birthday.

> *Venus her myrtle has, Phoebus his bays;*
> *Tea both excels which she vouchsafes to praise.*
> *The best of Queens and best of herbs we owe*
> *To that proud nation which the way did show*
> *To the fair region where the sun does rise;*
> *Whose rich productions we so justly prize.*
> *The Muse's friend, Tea, does our fancy aid,*
> *Repress those vapours which the head invade,*
> *And keep that palace of the soul serene,*
> *Fit on her birthday to salute the Queen.*[13]

With perception rare for a contemporary, Waller saw Catherine in historical perspective, as the link between England and the East, by accident of birth—not just as the royal sponsor of tea. As for Pepys, he saw little in the beverage, to him tea was still a medicine; for pleasure he preferred to look elsewhere.

He didn't have far to look in the London of the 1660s. Since the return of Charles II, both sexes, all classes, sought out pleasures long denied them under Cromwell. There were some that still enjoyed a mild game of shuffleboard, ninepins, or "bowls," but the temper of the majority was more bloodthirsty. Knife-slashing fights for prizes alternated with bear- or bull-baiting by dogs in the pit of Bear Garden, "a very rude and nasty pleasure"[14] to Pepys. Cockfights were a revived attraction. And, on occasion, crowds swarmed to watch a regicide "hanged, drawn, and quartered,"[15] just as casually as they attended Bartholomew Fair to see a rope dancer perform.

However, when there was a play at King's House, opened six months after the return of Charles, or at Covent Garden, which was new three years later, Pepys was there enjoying the enigma of masked and "beauty-spotted" ladies as much as the performance of the actors. Then when the weather grew warm, he went "by water to Fox-hall, and there walked in Spring Garden, [where] a man may go to spend what he will, or nothing, all is one. But to hear the nightingale and other birds, and hear fiddles, and there a harp, and here a Jew's trump, and here laughing, and there fine people walking, is mighty divertising."[16]

As the seventeenth century slipped into the eighteenth, men in every little hamlet preferred diversion in a coffeehouse. London by then had probably five hundred to choose from. Within noisy, smoky, crowded rooms, every class and calling sharpened wits on each other's abrasive tongue and whittled current convictions and suppositions into modern shape. Tea, and its effect on men's minds, morals, and manners, was a favorite controversial subject, which throughout the century satirists delighted to exaggerate.

Some, like John Wesley, at first considered tea in the same category as "strong drink." There were others who thought tea caused the "leathery, yellow look" of the Chinese; even agreed with Jonas Hanway that "Your very Chambermaids have lost their bloom, . . . by sipping tea."[17] But the majority of those who left their names to history listened to the learned physician Dr. Thomas Short when he recommended tea to "Gentlemen of a spritely Genius" who would "preserve the Continuance of their lively and distinct Ideas."[18]

For the moralists, tea was vindicated by mid-eighteenth century, when gin's consumption declined as tea's popularity rose. As for the chambermaids, it was Dr. Samuel Johnson, a self-confessed "hardened and shameless tea-drinker," who vigorously took issue with Mr. Hanway, in print. In the course of his defense of tea, Johnson cited his own imbibing, that he regularly "with tea amuses the evening, with tea solaces the midnight, and with tea welcomes the morning."[19] He, for one, was well aware of what Dr. Short had called the "eminent and unequalled Power" of tea. In fact, if Dr. Short's contentions were

54) Coffeehouse interior furnished with cane chairs, tall coffee pots, and customers drinking out of bowls called "dishes." Early 18th century. Woodcut from *Vulgus Britannicus*, 1775.

valid, then tea was the magic brew responsible for the intellectual brilliance of the eighteenth century, for he claimed that tea, besides its more obvious characteristics, "excites and sharpeneth the Thoughts, gives fresh Vigour and Force to Invention, awakens the Senses, and clears the Mind."[20]

Never for a moment would Catherine of Braganza have believed that any Englishman would ever so well regard the fragrant brew that made her think of home. Neither could she have imagined that of all the foreign oddities her dowry loosed on England, it would be tea which most affected English taste and habits.

So sweeping was the spell of tea and talk that, according to a contemporary, "every skettle-ally half a mile out of town was embellished with green arbours and shady retreats," and called a "Tea Garden." There in the semi-privacy of leafy niches, time was "beguiled with cakes and ale, tea and shrimp, strawberries and cream, syllabubs and junkets." No longer, as in the gardens of the Restoration, did speaking figures amaze the incredulous, nor *jets d'eau* soak the unwary to the raucous delight of onlookers. Garden statues now stood mute amid groups of grotesquely clipped shrubbery, while only the breeze whipped an occasional spray of water beyond the controlled plumes of a fountain. Music and fireworks, though, still provided entertainment for families on a holiday; for clandestine lovers lost in "mazes, lover's walks and woodbine bowers";[21] and for the world of fashion that on every fair day promenaded up and down or around the gravel paths to see and to be seen.

Fox-hall with its Spring Garden where Pepys found it "very pleasant and cheap going thither,"[22] grew into fashionable Vauxhall with twelve acres of celebrated gardens by the beginning of the eighteenth century. Mr. Spectator, Joseph Addison's fictitious personality, found them in 1712 still "exquisitely pleasant" as he strolled the paths with Sir Roger de Coverley. "When I considered the fragrancy of the walks and bowers, with the choirs of birds that sang upon the trees, and the loose tribe of people that walk under their shades, I could not but look upon the place as a kind of Mahometan paradise."[23] Through the glamorous years of the mid-eighteenth century, the place took on a special air of enchantment, particularly after dusk, for "when it grows dark the garden near the orchestre is illuminated, almost in an instant, with about 1500 glass lamps, which glitter among the trees, and render it exceeding light and brilliant."[24]

In such an atmosphere the parties at Vauxhall were very gay indeed, as that June evening in 1750 which Horace Walpole spent with friends "in our booth [where] we minced seven chickens into a china dish, which Lady Caroline stewed over a lamp with three parts of butter and a flagon of water, stirring, and rattling, and laughing, and we every minute expecting to have the dish fly about our ears . . ." The conversation that night, spiced with personal gossip and intimate play upon words in the manner of the times, "was no less lively than the whole transaction . . ." "In short," Walpole continues in his letter to George

55) Vauxhall Gardens, with its "walks and bowers" tucked between clipped trees, and its curving refreshment "booths" and orchestra pavilion rising in the foreground. Early 18th century.

Montagu, "the whole air of our party was sufficient, as you will easily imagine, to take up the whole attention of the garden; so much so, that from eleven o'clock till half an hour after one we had the whole concourse round our booth: at last, they came into the little gardens of each booth on the sides of ours . . ." It was a gala night, for "It was three o'clock before we got home."[25]

Walpole usually preferred Vauxhall, where "the garden is pleasanter, and one goes by water," to Ranelagh Gardens, which had opened in May 1742 after an outlay of £16,000. Walpole was there the night following the garden's spectacular debut, which he said had been attended by "the Prince, Princess, Duke, much nobility, and much mob besides." In a letter to his friend, Horace Mann, he described the place as having a "vast amphitheatre, finely gilt, painted, and illuminated, into which everybody that loves eating, drinking, staring, or crowding, is admitted for twelvepence." As a further inducement, the management promised: "Twice a-week there are to be ridottos [music and dancing], at guinea tickets, for which you are to have a supper and music."[26]

The chief attraction of Ranelagh was its "amphitheatre" built for concerts and promenading and called the "Rotunda." Besides housing a pipe organ as the backdrop of a four-tiered orchestra stage, the most spectacular feature was an enormous fireplace in the center of the circular building, its vast ornamental chimney stack rising to the roof of the galleried Rotunda. Ranelagh and Vauxhall were not to be equaled, not even in Europe, but many a smaller garden offered secluded bowers, mazes, and bordered walks, fireworks and music of sorts, and all included tea for the flash of a silver token at the gate, which admitted two persons at a cost of twelve shillings, more or less, for the season.

Gradually, as Tea Gardens became too popular, the *beau monde* withdrew into the privacy of its own homes and gardens. By mid-century, any gentleman who could speak of his land in acres had his own teahouse overlooking the most "pleasing prospect"; or his lady served tea to a select group of friends in the parlor, completely ignoring the controversy that raged around its merits. By that time, too, the equipment demanded by tea had found a pattern of its own, a combination of eastern form and western custom.

When Catherine first came to England, the gateleg table was the newest fashion. Bowls and trenchers, as large as two arms could encircle, still held the mounds of food set down at every meal. Thick, potent liquids swilled it down, drunk out of mug or tankard, two-handled cup or spouted posset pot. Coarse porous earthenware, burl wood, and stitched black leather were the common man's materials; while pewter, silver, a rare dish of faïence—or rarer still—some fragile Chinese porcelain, marked the home of wealth and of position. But even there, each guest must bring his table tools of fork and spoon—for forks were still a curiosity in England. As for equipment suitable for tea, none but that made in China was appropriate.

After Charles died and James II had fled England in undignified haste, there were close to fifty East India ships engaged in transforming the old English order of things. The revolution in politics that invited "Dutch" William and Mary, daughter of James, to the English throne, further accentuated the changes the East was imposing upon English style and fashion. For Mary, the new Queen, brought with her from Holland a taste for the same tea, porcelain, and lacquer-ware that Catherine had known in her youth in Portugal.

Since the early years of the seventeenth century, the Dutch had supplied northern Europe with the trade goods of the East. They had followed the Portuguese into the China Sea, and, by force, guile, and persuasion had established trading posts in a half-dozen contested, lucrative spots. By the beginning of the eighteenth century, after nearly a hundred years of sporadic and organized fighting in every sea lane around the globe by the European trespassers of Asia, the Portuguese had almost disappeared from Asia; the Dutch had lost practically all their holdings there; while the English remained in the East to exploit their gains.

At home, the motley assortment of eastern trade goods that poured with increasing volume from the holds of more and larger India ships was adapted and assimilated into the rapidly changing culture of England. By the time Anne succeeded her sister as Queen, the East had so revolutionized the habits of Englishmen that in 1710 *The Tatler** remarked that instead of "three rumps of beef" for breakfast as

---

* The Tatler, *written by Sir Richard Steele (1672–1729), was published three times a week in London from April 1709 to January 1711. It contained political and social gossip and occasionally essays on the manners and morals of the time.*

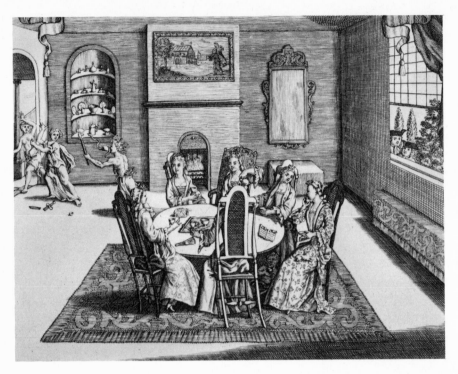

56) "The Tea-Table." Ladies in calico gowns sit on high-back cane Restoration chairs drinking the newly fashionable Chinese tea. A satirical print sold by John Bowles at Cornhill, London, c. 1710.

in the time of Queen Elizabeth, "tea and bread and butter . . . have prevailed of late years."[27]

Tea, from being a medicine, had become a fashion. Not only had it changed the breakfast menu, but around tea and the tea table now revolved a new kind of social life. Gone were the days when King and court ate, drank, and made love openly for public entertainment. Anne, even though the daughter of James II, was a domestic soul. She held her court across the silver of her tea table, instead of in the shadow of a bed made of the metal, as had been the French court custom of the previous generation of monarchs. In imitation of Anne, every fashionable female in England sipped Chinese tea from tiny Chinese porcelain bowls and ordered one of the new tea tables from which to serve it.

Trays of some sort, under different names, in varying shapes and sizes, have always been used to serve food and drink. At the time of the

Restoration, the salver was that "new fashioned peece of wrought plate, broad and flat, with a foot underneath, . . . used in giving Beer, or other liquid thing to save the Carpit or Cloaths from drops."[28] Fifty years later under Anne, a waiter of silver was "new fashioned" for tea. Round or square, on three short feet or four, contemporaries called it a "tea-board," or "tea-table." By the middle of the century, additional tea things doubled the size of the silver tea board. In opulent households, an especially large silver tray with feet might rest on its own

57) "Family Group" (c. 1730). An early 18th-century painting of a family around a tea table, by Gawen Hamilton (1697–1737).

stand made of wood, the tray's tiny silver feet sunk into little hollows cut into the wooden top of the stand.

Joiners, who worked in walnut or the new mahogany recently introduced from the West Indies, made tray-top tables for the hostess; and for each guest a little tripod table, just large enough to hold a single cup. These were "teapoys," an English mutilation of eastern words for "three-foot," which had followed tea to England. In the second half of the eighteenth century, tripod tables grew in size until some could accommodate as many as twelve cups and saucers, one in each deep scallop of the perimeter. As for rectangular tea tables, they were surrounded by a little fence of Chinese fretwork to keep tea things from sliding off. Depending upon the kind of tea things, they were called "silver," or "china" tables, one being as precious as the other.

Much of the early value of Chinese procelain lay in its mystery to the West. At the beginning of the eighteenth century, no one in England or on the Continent had yet fathomed the tantalizing enigma of its composition. As one tea-drinking Queen after another increased public demand for more porcelain tea things than either the overloaded East India ships or the attempts of local potters at imitation could supply, goldsmiths—who worked in both silver and gold and followed every whim of fashion—made English translations of Chinese teaware in silver.

Teapots, round or pear-shaped like a flat-bottomed gourd; high-shouldered little cans in which to keep the precious tea; even tiny, handleless cups of silver—all traditional Chinese shapes that changed but little under English hands—were the first native attempts at new forms as new to England as the recently transplanted ritual of tea. At first, English pots were small as in China, not that each guest poured her own tea as in China, but rather because tea was scarce in England, and expensive. For the same English reason, early tea canisters held only five or six ounces and were locked in a chest as a protection against filching fingers.

Cups of silver, however, proved hard and hot to the touch and those of native pottery thick and clumsy; only cups of Chinese porcelain, smooth as vitreous satin, complemented the drink. In China, at this time, tea bowls had no handles, but had covers to keep the whisked tea hot while steeping. For export, the Chinese revived their ancient prac-

58) "Tea Party" (c. 1725). English oil painting by an unknown artist, which gives a good idea of the tea equipment of the time. On the left is the sugar bowl with its leaning lid; next, a hexagonal tea canister, covered hot-milk jug, and a fluted voiding bowl for the dregs; and in the foreground, what might be the bowl's cover used as a spoon tray, and sugar tongs shaped like fire tongs. On the right stands a squat pyriform teapot not much larger than the handleless cups of Chinese porcelain held in approved fashion. The Sign of the Golden Ball, Colonial Williamsburg.

tice of attaching handles to their cups—cups so small that the tea in two or three of them would barely fill one western cup today. On English tea tables, Chinese teacup covers became English saucers, and the imported combination was familiarly spoken of as made of *china*, still the English synonym for porcelain.

Now, proportionate teaspoons of silver were a necessity, for the day had long since past when one seven-inch spoon performed all table operations. Necessity also invented the mote skimmer, which with its perforated bowl skimmed bits of floating twig or dried beetle out of the tea, and with its slender spike handle picked away uncurled tea leaves that clogged the teapot spout.

As for milk and sugar, with which no Chinaman ever adulterated tea, unrelated jugs and pitchers, boxes, baskets, and bowls were used for several decades before fashion demanded that these echo the shape of the teapot. Sugar was a luxury in England; honey was the common sweetener when Catherine sailed from Portugal with sugar for ballast instead of promised dowry bullion. By the end of the seventeenth century, 10,000 tons of sugar on an average were yearly imported from India and the East, contrasted to the less than 88 tons in 1665. By the eighteenth century, round-topped cones of loaf sugar were commonplace in every English kitchen, hacked into jagged chunks for the table by steel nippers that resembled iceman's tongs. But on the tea table, sugar tongs were of silver—fragile scissors with wide, slightly cupped ends, and later U-shaped bands of springy metal. Either way, in all their dainty uselessness, they were a symbol of the extravagant elegance tea and porcelain had brought to the English table. Even the notoriously unkempt Dr. Samuel Johnson expected tongs among the "common decencies" of a tea table.

Over this collection of almost miniature tea things towered the tea kettle on its stand. Kept indifferently hot by a spirit lamp, the kettle, a large-size copy of a teapot, generously watered the bit of precious tea in the pot until tea flowed as freely as talk and spawned "visiting days." These, according to *The Tatler*, were conceived "to pass away that odious thing called *time*, in discourses too trivial to raise any *reflections* which may put well-bred persons to the trouble of thinking."[29]

"Visits" of Queen Anne's England, even though circumscribed as much by etiquette as was the aesthetic tea ceremony of the East, offered

59) Dr. Samuel Johnson at the home of Mr. and Mrs. Boswell, as he "with tea solaces the midnight." The tea tray is complete with a small straight-sided teapot, huge urn for hot water, and the "common decency" of sugar tongs. Caricature from James Boswell's *Journal of a Tour to the Hebrides,* 1786. Engraved by Collings and Rowlandson.

excitement in their formula of "a sip of Tea, then for a draught or two of Scandal to digest it, . . . till the half hour's past, and [callers] have disburthen'd themselves of their Secrets, and take Coach for some other place to collect new matter for Defamation."[30] In other circles, at a later time, teas were more leisurely lionizing affairs, as was the one of Samuel Johnson's story, in which he tells of "the lady [who] asked me for no other purpose but to make a zany of me, and set me gabbling to a parcel of people I knew nothing of. So I had my revenge of her; for I swallowed five and twenty cups of her tea, and did not treat her to as many words."[31]

It may have been just "tea" to the doctor, but to his hostess in the 1750s, it was a blend of green tea at 12s. a pound, Hyson at 15s., and

60) "The Old Maid." She sips her dish of tea in solitary grandeur, her teapot on its trivet and the kettle on its stand. English print, 1777.

Bohea from 30s. to 35s. Thirty-five shillings then was much more than our present $4.90; it was a craftsman's wage for a week. At the same time in China, tea drinkers bought a pound of "fragrant leaves," "lotus heart," "jade milk," or "holy dew," for a single shilling.

The mighty East India Company, whose sailing freighters were now significantly "Tea Waggons," paid no more. Tea was their staple; tea was their monopoly; tea was their treasure. So it was also to the Crown, for every pound was taxed 5s., plus 5 percent *ad valorem*; under the Georges, it was raised to 1s., plus 50 percent tax on estimated value. Steadily the shipments increased after 1750 from three to over ten million pounds a year, estimated sufficient for each Englishman to drink tea at least once a day. Every Englishman did—"nay, farmer's servants even demanding tea for their breakfast, with the maids."[32] The poor, too, insisted on tea, in spite of being warned that "the yearly expense of tea, sugar, &c, for two persons, exceeds that of the necessary article of bread, sufficient for a family of five persons."[33]

All, however, was not English revenue. William Pitt, "The Great Commoner," calculated that less than half the tea consumed paid duty. The rest was smuggled in from Holland by "honest" smugglers, protected and patronized by the most respectable segments of society.

Parson Woodforde felt no embarrassment when "Andrews the smuggler brought me this night about 11 o'clock a bagg of Hyson tea."[34] And the well-connected Mrs. Elizabeth Montagu drank her "couple of pounds of good smuggled tea . . . with a safe conscience . . ."[35] Even at that, tea was not cheap, but it was plentiful.

All over England, frugal housewives stretched their supply with "smouch" of dried leaves or leaf buds dyed with molasses, clay, log-wood, or worse, even though fleets of smuggled tea and Company ware-houses bulged with the stuff. Or they bought used tea leaves from the cooks of the wealthy, brewed them until there was no color left in them, then ate the leaves on bread and butter, sprinkled over with a little sugar.

The spiraling trade of the East India Company had scattered far social amenities unknown to the fathers of most eighteenth-century Englishmen, at the same time achieving through tea, that "politer way of living" John Evelyn had glimpsed at its beginning. Tea furniture— all the accouterments attached to the ritual of serving tea, whether of silver, clay, or wood—recorded in the round every innovation, every change of status, every whim of fashion of a mercurial century. As wealth and the supply of tea increased, tea things continued to register the affluence.

Canisters, once so small, doubled in size. The tea chest that formerly held a pair of canisters plus a bowl for sugar or for blending tea, was itself filled with tea and called a "caddy"—a word picked bodily out of the idiom of eastern trade, where a kati was 16 tael, a Chinese pound, as tea was weighed and sold. Teapots, too, were twice as large as those of Queen Anne's day, and now were matched by the rest of the tea equipage, the fashionable term for tea things. Then for those frequent gatherings of the talented and the brilliant that "enlightened" the eighteenth century, a colossal tea urn, instead of a kettle, ran either hot water or tea at the turn of a spigot.

By the 1760s, even the petty controversies that formerly had swirled around tea, blew up into storms that raged high into circles of finance and government. Conquests in India and politics at home now made the interests of Parliament synonymous with those of the East India Com-pany. Both of these institutions pyramided their credit and their policies on tea, so that the future of each hinged on that of the other. With some

61) "The Tea Tax Tempest." Father Time with his magic lantern shows to the Four Continents the explosion of the teapot which routed the British on one side, and on the other tossed the Liberty Cap within reach of the Americans. By Karl Guttenberg of Nuremberg, 1778.

pride, tempered by a sense of foreboding shared by many of his contemporaries, Horace Walpole wrote in 1768: "The immense wealth that had flowed into the country from . . . the East Indies, bore down all barriers of economy, and introduced a luxury of expense unknown to empires of vaster extent."[36]

This was the "enough"—"rather wished than hoped for"—that Edward Hyde, Lord Chancellor to Charles II, had recognized in the dowry of Catherine of Braganza, when in 1661 he wrote: "The truth is, there is enough in that Treaty, . . . to render that allyance very popular." He argued then that "besydes the portion in money, which . . . I belieue much more then could be had any wher else, that advantages and benefitts to trade make the marchants most enamoured on it; and sure wee have very ill luk if, in the East and West Indyes, they do not make incredible benefitt by the concessyons, even to their owne heartes desyre."[37]

Greed of the Company, and the shortsightedness of George III and his ministers, shriveled those "incredible benefitts." Stubborn Englishmen on both sides of the Atlantic refused on principle to pay the offensive duties on tea. By 1772, there was an estimated three years' supply spoiling in Company warehouses, "and other India goods . . . to the amount of four millions, as some say."[38] As debts and dividends remained unpaid, East India stock tumbled from two hundred and eighty to a disastrous one hundred and sixty, at which point the Company was relieved of paying the government the four hundred thousand pounds a year it "had offered, in consideration of certain new advantages granted them in their tea-trade."[39]

Of tea there was now a plenty. Actually, both the Company and the Empire were cracking under the strain of its surplus weight. But casual visitors to England, such as the Duc de la Rochefoucauld, saw only that tea provided those it had made rich "with an opportunity to display their magnificence in the matter of teapots, cups and so on."[40]

CHAPTER EIGHT

The Porcelain Mystery

Porcelain *"is of far higher price than gold, inasmuch as one rarely finds any of the true material, and much that is sold is unreal."*[1]

—GUIDO PANCIROLLI*

THE century that flowed to a crest on tea made a fetish of porcelain. "Teapots, cups and so on" of the eighteenth century stood as fragile monuments to a romantic success story whose beginnings lay buried in the fables and mythology of the East; for Chinese porcelain, the "true material"—smooth, clean, and white—was a substance that for years no one in Europe could explain, except in terms of the supernatural.

From the beginning of history, there had been potters who shaped local clays into vessels of necessity. Yet no matter how skilled the craftsman, nor whether his wares were sun-baked, or kiln-fired, they were thick, coarse, porous, and their colors were determined by the earth from which they were made. Only a glaze of either opaque tin oxide, or poisonous lead, kept liquids from dissolving them.

By comparison, the first pieces of porcelain to reach Europe, carried across two continents by foot-weary crusaders, by traders and missionaries on camel back, inspired fantastic stories of mysterious origin. Centuries before the Portuguese rounded the tip of Africa, Marco Polo,

* Guido Pancirolli (1523–99) was a noted Italian scholar and jurist.

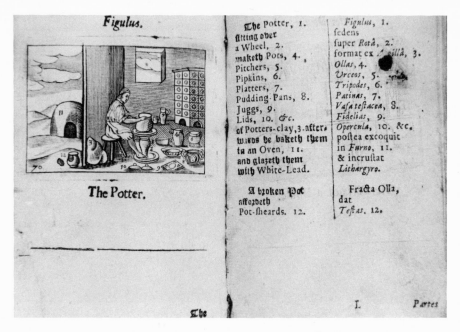

62) The craft of the potter has changed but little in a thousand years. A double page, in both English and Latin, from *Orbis Sensualium Pictus* (*The Visible World*), by Johann Amos Comenius, 1672.

from what he had seen added to the little he was told, described how the Chinese manufactured "cups or bowls and dishes of porcelainware." He said: "They collect a certain kind of earth, as it were, from a mine, and laying it in a great heap, suffer it to be exposed to the wind, the rain, and the sun, for thirty or forty years, during which time it is never disturbed. By this it becomes refined and fit for being wrought into the vessels above mentioned. Such colours as may be thought proper are then laid on, and the ware is afterwards baked in ovens or furnaces. Those persons, therefore, who cause the earth to be dug, collect it for their children and grandchildren."[2]

Two centuries of fanciful elaboration embroidered this naïve account into the complicated formula of Guido Pancirolli, which later, in 1617, was translated from the Latin into French and circulated throughout Europe. It began: "Past centuries have not seen porcelains, which are merely a certain mass composed of plaster, eggs, scales of marine locusts and other similar kinds, which mass being well united and worked to-

63) "Preparations of Ingredients in Mortars Run by Water Power." A Chinese watercolor from *The Manufacture of Porcelain.*

64) "Forming the Ware by Hand." Chinese watercolor from *The Manufacture of Porcelain.*

65) Pou-tai, also spelled Pû-Sa, Chinese god of
Contentment, the personification of sensualism,
and as such also considered the god of porcelain.
From an old print in *History of the Ceramic Art*
by Albert Jacquemart, 1877.

gether, is secretly hidden underground by the father of a family, who
informs his children alone of it."[3]

Much as the "heap" of Marco Polo, this mixture, if left undisturbed
for eighty years, promised patient descendants and heirs vast profits in
vessels "beautiful to the sight in form and colour," vessels which quite
possibly might resemble some kind of alabaster. But for Renaissance
Italy, the greatest virtue of "porcelain" so made lay in the belief that
"inasmuch as if one puts poison into one of these vessels it breaks immediately."[4]

This was the same faith the Chinese had in their "false jade," their
celadon. And it may well have been this "virtue" that prompted the
Grand Duke Francesco Maria de' Medici,* with his passion for chemistry and the arts, to pursue his experiments in quest of the true nature of
porcelain, for he lived in the treacherously uncertain society of sixteenth-century Italy. Whatever the reason, by 1575 he had succeeded in
producing the first porcelain of sorts in all of Europe. Today there are
still about forty pieces of attributed de' Medici porcelain in the world,
five in the Metropolitan Museum of Art in New York. More than a
century was to elapse before another princeling-sponsored porcelain
enterprise would actually discover the secret of the "true material."

* *Francesco Maria de' Medici (1541–87). Francesco I, Grand Duke of Tuscany,
despotic and lustful, was son and heir of Cosimo de' Medici.*

Porcelain, and possibly also its legends, had long been known to adventuring, free-lancing sailors. In fact, it was those that first knew the East Indies who gave porcelain its euphonious name, for they thought it as lustrous and valuable as cowrie shells—the medium of exchange in that part of the world—which they fondly called *porcella,* a diminutive of *porca* in Italian and Portuguese. When Vasco da Gama returned to Portugal in 1499, after his first glimpse of the continent Marco Polo had described, porcelains were among the exotic gifts he brought his King, samples of the strange wonders of the East.

In the opulent years that followed, the Portuguese carracks that sailed the Grand Trade route from Canton to Lisbon carried up to one third of their cargo in Chinese porcelains. Even though the Portuguese had been barred from Canton proper following their first ill-considered salvo, after 1557 they were permitted twice a year, in June and January, to leave their perch on rocky Macao to bargain for porcelains and other curiosities at the great trade sales in Canton. Half a world away in Lisbon, no less than six shops in one street alone sold the porcelains of China, not only to their own countrymen but to the traveling merchants of half of Europe. So it was that by the time Catherine of Braganza became Queen of England, a century of porcelain in Portugal had made it for her almost a commonplace.

In 1558, one year after the Portuguese had established trade with Canton, Elizabeth I ascended the throne of England; but it was not until forty-two years later that she chartered The Governour and Merchants of London Trading into the East Indies. When Catherine arrived as Queen, neither Hampton Court nor Whitehall had enough of the fragile stuff even to mention it. The "Portingall cuppes" Charles I valued among his plate had vanished with his other treasures. England in the 1660s was a rugged earthy place. Beer and ale still overflowed mugs of leather, wood, or coconut shell—plain or silver-bound—and foamed across long tables hewn of oak, while lips more finical were served with pewter, silver, or Venetian glass. None of these though, not even native crockery, was congenial to the foreign herb recently introduced as "tea." In leather, wood, or coconut shell, tea surely must have been a bitter brew; nor was it much less a medicine in pewter, glass, or silver. Within one short generation, however, the porcelain of Catherine's childhood, with its roots in the same ancient soil of China as those of

66) Búcaro, traditional Chinese I-hsing stoneware ranging in color from sandy to red and brown, and in date from Yung-cheng (1723–35)—the right-hand pot of the center foreground group of three—through the 18th century.

tea, turned tea into a palatable pleasure for Englishmen and made it the money-cargo of the East India Company.

Not for itself, however, was the first venture porcelain sent to England; but rather it acted as ballast and at the same time raised chests of tea out of the swashing bilge water of a long year's voyage. In the eyes of the Company, porcelain was never anything more than a necessary, although pleasant, adjunct to their money-cargo of tea. But in China, men valued the fired product of their native earth for aesthetic reasons, such as its age, the barely perceptible patina acquired from the caresses of a thousand hands, or for the aura of association that surrounded a piece which had once belonged to some celebrity. In addition, line and color spoke with meaning to the tutored eye, and the ear of the connoisseur listened with appreciation to the resonance of porcelain, the tone of which varied with the size, shape, and quality of the piece. It was only in the West that the attribute of translucence was subsequently added as a requisite of porcelain.

Much of the tea-ware, though, that paved the holds as ballast of seventeenth-century East India ships came from the kilns of I-hsing near Shanghai and had still another quality. Besides its earth-red color, the old books tell of its "musky odour"—a faint volatile fragrance vaguely suggestive of geranium leaf or an aromatic carnation—said to give a special flavor to the tea. The Portuguese called it "búcaro ware," *búcaro* being a "sweet-smelling earth," especially aromatic when wet. It was

67) English tea canister of unglazed red stoneware with a silver cover. Four inches tall with flat sides decorated with chinoiserie motifs, it is attributed to John Philip Elers. Late 17th or early 18th century.

68) English teapot of unglazed red stoneware with recessed panels of unfired gilding decorated with applied bits of chinoiserie. It measures 4⅛ inches to the top of its gilt lion finial. Attributed to John Philip Elers. Late 17th century.

"red porcelain" to Englishmen—fine, hard, red clay, fired to a resonance, and polished to a glow on a lathe. To the potters of Staffordshire, it was a challenge, for they had red clay right at their doorstep.

Among those attracted by the red clay of Staffordshire were the brothers David and John Phillip Elers, who in their youth had been both potters and silversmiths somewhere along the Rhine. With their sensitive artisan's touch, equal to the skill born into eastern hands through generations, they modeled red teaware with sprigs of plum blossoms comparable to the Chinese. The fame of the "Potteries" of Staffordshire spread now well beyond sight of its billows of black smoke. Hardy travelers urged their stumbling horses over incredible roads riddled with "pot-holes," some deep enough to drown a man, just "to see the making of fine teapotts, cups and saucers of fine red earth, in imitation and as curious as that which comes from China."[5] All, however, shared the illusion that the fine red stoneware they called "red porcelain" was but a colored variation of the enigmatic white import Englishmen dubbed "chinaware."

Just as an assortment of Portuguese artisans had followed Catherine to England, so men skilled in the arts and crafts as practiced in Holland crossed the channel in 1688 with William and Mary. Holland, which for centuries had transported the commerce of much of the western world, had kept for herself choice bits of eastern goods as they passed through her markets. Of Chinese porcelain she preferred the clean blue and white wares of the Ming dynasty, which ended in 1644—by which time the hands of Dutch potters had learned to shape their own soft dark earthenware in the image of Chinese models, an art the Portuguese had already practiced for all of fifty years. Thick native earthenware was freely coated with an opaque glaze of white tin enamel, then decorated in cobalt blue in the manner of Ming porcelains. In Portugal, it was "faïence," but we now call tin-enameled Dutch facsimiles of real porcelain "delft."

Porcelain, even delft, was a passion with Mary, which she had acquired while living in Holland. A little more than ten years before when she bid Catherine good-bye in 1677, Mary had wept on leaving home to accompany her new husband, William of Orange, to Holland. Catherine had then assured her that she knew well the qualms of royal princesses when they married, for Catherine had never seen Charles II at the time she left Portugal to be his bride. "But, Madam, you came into England, I am leaving England!"[6] had been Mary's indignant rejoinder. Now, in 1688, both Mary and her husband were triumphantly back in England to share the throne her father, James II, had hastily abandoned. And Catherine, the Queen-Dowager, was still trying to return to her beloved Portugal, which political conniving would not allow until the spring of 1692.

By then, the "noble pile"[7] of Hampton Court which first received

Catherine in a farthingale was being enlarged by Christopher Wren into a quadrangle of "most beautiful form"—all but the Water Gallery down by the river, which Mary saved for herself from William's renovating hand. There, according to Daniel Defoe, "she order'd all the neat little curious things to be done, . . . and made it the pleasantest little thing within doors that could possibly be made, . . ."[8]

Mary loved that "private retreat" of hers. It became so much a part of her that when she died William couldn't bear the sight of it and tore it down. But during her lifetime, the Water Gallery was filled with her collection of delft and a "vast stock of fine China ware, the like whereof was not then to be seen in England; . . ." Defoe remembered that even the "long gallery . . . was fill'd with this china, and every other place where it could be plac'd with advantage."[9]

Daniel Defoe was known in his time for much more than inventing Robinson Crusoe. After failing as a commission merchant in Spanish and Portuguese goods, and as a tile manufacturer, he started in 1704 a tri-weekly news sheet called *The Review*. As one of the many satirical pamphleteers, who were in fact eighteenth-century England's news editors and commentators, Defoe was in perpetual political hot water; yet his sharp mind never missed an opportunity to describe a new trade, nor to comment on a new fashion.

The "custom or humor . . . of furnishing houses with china-ware," which Defoe talked about, Mary had caught in Holland from a French Huguenot named Daniel Marot, who had been an architect in France before Louis XIV revoked the Edict of Nantes. On the Continent Marot had designed spectacular "Porcelain Rooms," stacked to the rafters with trade porcelains from the East and delft from Dutch kilns. With Mary's imported "china-mania," Marot's ideas spread throughout England before the eighteenth century had properly begun, until the wives of stolid Englishmen were "piling their china upon the tops of cabinets, scrutoires, and every chymney-piece, to the tops of the ceilings, . . ."[10]

"Scrutoires" and "chymney-pieces" were as new to England as china-ware. Mantel shelves and brackets were replacing the old projecting, rounded bolection moldings around fireplaces; and scrutoires—anglicized from the Portuguese *escritorio*—were new-fashioned writing desks. Even cabinets had changed. Many now had glass doors to display their

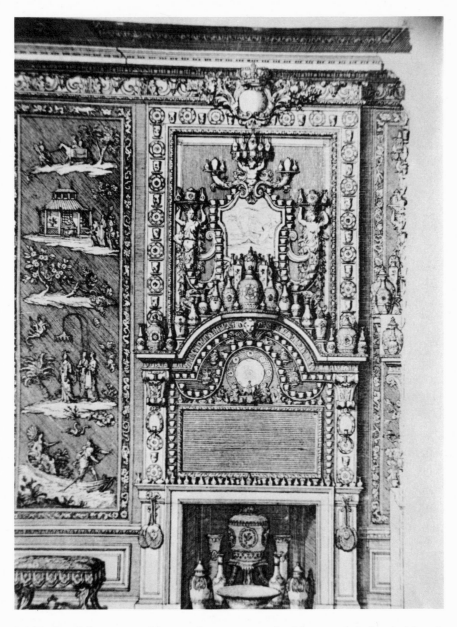

69) Early 18th-century chimney breast covered with porcelain-loaded brackets and edged with alternating cups and saucers. The mantel shelf and fireplace opening are crowded with vases, and rows of tiny bowls are crammed in between. From *Das Ornament Werk des Daniel Marot*, Vol. II, by Ernst Wasmuth, 1892.

70) Garniture of Chinese blue and white covered vases and beakers, shapes and decorations that were repeatedly borrowed by western craftsmen. K'ang Hsi period (1662–1722).

china contents and stood almost twice as tall as those Catherine had brought with her to England. But now each shelf and cabinet was crowded with collections of chinaware "till it became a grievance in the expense of it, and even injurious to their families and estates."[11] Fifty years before, almost the same words had decried comparable extravagance in the Portugal of Catherine's youth—"buffets, handsome desks, chairs, wardrobes, chests of tortoise-shell, plain and wrought services, China and Japan wares were so many excuses for huge sums being lavishly spent."[12] The mania had caught up with England.

The fad for porcelain had been a full generation a-brewing. The very year, 1662, that Catherine, Infanta of Portugal, sailed as Queen to England with Bombay in her dowry, K'ang Hsi was proclaimed Emperor of China on the other side of the world. Even while the Portuguese on Macao were paying an exorbitant tribute to him, the Portuguese in Bombay reluctantly turned over their jewel of the Indian Ocean to the English. In the thirty odd years that followed, an occasional English East India ship in search of tea touched the ports of China—Chusan, Amoy, even Canton—with precarious success. Then in the closing months of the fabulous seventeenth century, K'ang Hsi opened a limited bit of Canton to the "red-haired devils" from England, over the violent objections of the Portuguese on Macao.

Notwithstanding the "many troubles and vexations . . . from these subtile Chineese," the little English galley *Macclesfield* on the spot managed to load a cargo that glowed and breathed of the East. One hundred thousand fans in boxes and chests of silk (raw and wrought) shouldered tubs of chinaware of varying sizes; while 120 piculs* of brass cash—"a sort of small money formerly curr^t in y^s place, but now dry'd downe"—tinkled every time the ship rolled. Occasionally, a finger of stray sunlight touched the mother-of-pearl inlaid in a tea table, any one of three hundred nests of six, or shimmered a dull silvery gleam from a tutenag† canister of tea, bright enough to rival the shine on the ingots of gold. Over all, the hot smells from the hold—of pitch and tar and stagnant bilge water—were more or less submerged by the lingering fragrance of musk spiced prickly with pepper.[13]

These were the tokens of two hundred years of Portuguese adventuring in the East that late in 1699 crammed the creaking, groaning hulk of the 250-ton English galley at Canton. Everything was there—from the pepper (1000 piculs of it), which first sent Renaissance Christians around the world—to the tea, tea tables, and chinaware that ushered in the promise of an elegant eighteenth century. These were surely "advantages and benefitts of trade"[14] beyond even those anticipated from Catherine's dowry by the farsighted Edward Hyde, who had been much more than Lord Chancellor to Charles II.

Ever since Charles was Prince of Wales in exile, and Hyde his guardian, he had been an old and trusted friend of the future monarch. With the Restoration, which was a political triumph for Hyde, Charles made him Viscount Cornbury and Earl of Clarendon. It was Hyde who from the beginning championed Catherine at court, envisioned a trade empire in her dowry, and acted as the kind, wise counselor during those difficult early years of her marriage. His own daughter, Anne, had in 1660 secretly married Charles's brother, the Duke of York, later James II. Their two daughters, Mary and Anne, were both eventually

* *An Asian measure of weight equal to 100 kati, or 133⅓ pounds avoirdupois.*
† *Tutenag was the name loosely applied in the India trade to zinc; but technically it was an eastern alloy of copper, zinc, and nickel, resembling a whitish pewter.*

queens of England. So it was Edward Hyde's granddaughter Mary who now ruled England with her husband William of Orange—now at the turn of the century when Catherine's dowry was coming into the fullness of its promise. It only remained for Englishmen to assimilate the exotic abundance.

Chinaware they took promptly to their hearts. When short of money, even old clothes were bartered for what Joseph Addison of *The Spectator* fame called "brittle ware." He swore he had "known an old petticoat metamorphosed into a punch-bowl, and a pair of breeches into a tea-pot." And he told how his "friend Tradewell . . . calls his great room, that is nobly furnished with china, his wife's wardrobe. 'In yonder corner,' says he [Tradewell], 'are about twenty suits of clothes, and on that scrutoire above a hundred yards of furbelowed silk.' " All this, said Addison, was "a kind of ostentation" of wealth. However, he added: "Did our women take delight in heaping up piles of earthen platters, brown jugs, and the like useful products of our British potteries, there would be some sense in it."[15]

The best the British potteries could then do was to cover their brown earthenware with a light-colored slip—but everyone knew that wasn't porcelain. Neither was the red teaware of Staffordshire. No one yet had found "in England beds of porcelain, such as they have in China," which early in the seventeenth century scientifically minded Sir Francis Bacon had described as "a kind of plaster buried in the earth and by length of time congealed and glazed into that fine substance; . . . ,"[16] much as his contemporary Pancirolli had done. Both of these men were scholars and jurists of keen perception, far more learned than most, yet neither knew a better explanation for porcelain. In fact, as late as the 1818 edition of Dr. Samuel Johnson's *Dictionary,* the word *porcelain* was still "said to be derived from *pour cent années;* because it was believed by Europeans, that the materials . . . were matured under ground one hundred years."

However, those Europeans who avidly outbid each other for the thin trickle of Chinese porcelains that survived the accidents of transport cared little for the mysteries of its making. Gold was their problem— gold enough to buy more porcelains. In the princeling courts of Europe, one was as precious as the other.

Augustus the Strong, Elector of Saxony, being short of gold, actually bartered 600 dragoons (mounted infantry) to the King of Prussia for an even greater number of Chinese porcelains—including the famous eighteen so-called "Dragon" vases, of which fourteen can still be seen in the *Staatliche Kunstsammlungen* in Dresden. Some time before, in 1701, to satisfy the same expensive passion, he had practically kidnapped from the King of Prussia the young apothecary's apprentice, Johann Böttger, who had early acquired a reputation for alchemy.

Alchemy, the chemistry of the Middle Ages, is surrounded by legends, one of which credits its founding to the Egyptian god Hermes, or Thoth, whose name is perpetuated to this day in vessels "hermetically" sealed. And today, too, in the Leyden Museum are still a number of papyri written in Greek before the third century A.D. which preserve, among other evidence of ancient knowledge, recipes for the manufacture of base metals into alloys that would simulate gold. These were originally written as manuals for those artisans who fashioned imitation jewelry, but through repeated successes became eventually to be regarded as reliable formulae for the transmutation of metals into real gold. In

71) "The Alchemist at Work." Attributed to Pieter Breughel the Elder, c. 1558.

addition, oriental magic and astrology from the East, carried to Europe by Arabs through Spain, had adulterated the serious early investigations into systematic chemistry, which had previously been held as a secret monopoly within the tight circle of the priestly caste. The resulting alchemistical precepts were transmitted generation by generation not just through books, but more commonly in closely held family recipes and by the repeated traditional processes used by artisans, such as jewelers, painters, workers in glass and in pottery. By the sixteenth century, a few chemically minded scientists of that disease-ridden age began to concern themselves with medicinal cures, with finding the "Elixir of Life," but many continued to struggle with the transmutation of base metals into gold.

One such was Johann Böttger. Yet even though he was held virtually a prisoner for six years by Augustus the Strong of Saxony—first at Dresden, then at Meissen farther along the Elbe—neither threats nor punishment inspired him to conjure gold from his secret powders and tinctures. Ensconced in the King's castle laboratory, appropriately called the *Goldhaus,* Böttger was surrounded with every luxury except freedom. Only Ehrenfried Walther von Tschirnhausen, first alchemist to Augustus, was his friend and advisor.

Ever since von Tschirnhausen had been in need of a crucible that would not collapse its contents of alloys into the fire when the temperature was raised dangerously high by the bellows, he had dabbled in ceramics. Every likely bit of rock or clay he found went into his pockets and those of his servants and burdened his carriage as he wandered the countryside. The floor of his laboratory was a clutter of ten years of collecting when in 1704 Böttger arrived. By 1708, the year von Tschirnhausen died, their combined skills had produced "red porcelain" to equal the Chinese; but more important still, Böttger had been convinced that there was more "gold" in porcelain of the sort Augustus would appreciate than in all the potions of alchemy.

By its very nature, porcelain intrigued the scientists of the seventeenth and eighteenth centuries—the apothecaries and doctors, the glass chemists and alchemists—those who explored the ancient philosophical elements of earth, water, air, and fire, of which porcelain was made. For Chinese porcelain was of a very special kind of earth. It was a mixture of the whitest so-called "china-clay" and "china-stone," whose hard powdered particles would vitrify only at a temperature much higher than was possible in an ordinary potter's kiln.

So much was first deduced by Böttger at Meissen. But only a lucky fluke at the right time brought him the necessary china-clay. A nearby hammersmith had found some sticky white mud in the shoes of his horse, which he sold at the Saxon court as hair powder to whiten the wigs then in fashion. He vaguely hoped it would make him a fortune. As a matter of fact, as an ingredient of porcelain, it revolutionized an age.

Not until a year or more later, in 1712, did Père d'Entrecolles send back home to France the first description of how the Chinese in his parish of Ching-tê Chên actually made their porcelain. He wrote in French and spelled phonetically the Chinese name of "china-clay" as *kaolin,* and "china-stone" as *petuntse.* But at Ching-tê Chên, the great porcelain town of a "million souls" and three thousand furnaces, it was *pai-tun-tzŭ,* meaning in Mandarin "white-stone-[for]-porcelain," and *kao ling* for "high hill," where up river in the next province time

72) "Open Furnaces." A Chinese watercolor from *The Manufacture of Porcelain.* Artist unknown.

73) "Inspecting and Packing." A Chinese watercolor from *The Manufacture of Porcelain*. Artist unknown.

had weathered *pai-tun-tzŭ* into a fine white china-clay. The two, in varying proportions, were kneaded with pure mountain spring water into a plastic dough by dozens of bare yellow trampling feet. Then slabs of the mix were rolled and pummeled until no tiny air hole, nor hair, nor grain of sand, remained to spoil the ware.[17]

From this, plates and bowls were turned upon a wheel, or nimble fingers "figured" bits of clay into fantastic forms. By the time a piece was stacked into the kiln, some seventy pairs of hands had shared its making. The heat from burning straw and wood now rose by degrees to an inferno of as much as 1500 degrees centigrade, until—seen through the peephole—plates, bowls, and whimsicals seemed consumed in the blinding roseate glow of the kiln's interior. That was the moment of fusion, as if the "finger of God" actually had touched them, as many believed. The fire died out, the porcelain cooled in the kiln, but in their bath of fire some had warped, some had cracked, and all had shrunk from 12 to 25 percent. A perfect piece was virtually a miracle.

In the West, rapture for porcelain grew with the eighteenth century.

But the prime English reason for importing Chinese porcelain was the fashion for tea. Nothing but cups, one hundred thousand of them, was the chinaware ballast of the *Trumbull* galley that "saved the monsoon"* the season after the *Macclesfield*. When Mary's sister Anne inherited the throne, "China vessels [were] playthings for women of all ages. An old lady of fourscore [kept] as busy in cleaning an Indian mandarin, as her great grand-daughter . . . in dressing her baby."[18] By mid-century, the eight or so English square-riggers that loaded at Canton, even though no larger than 499 "tons burthen" (to avoid carrying a chaplain), paved their holds with one hundred and fifty, some with two hundred, chests of chinaware that averaged six hundred pieces packed in sago.

In London, at the India Warehouse in Leadenhall Street, one exotic lot after another was sold at candle-auction each time one measured inch of candle burned through spirited bidding down to a sputtering end. The broken and damaged porcelain leftovers were later advertised as "extremely Cheap, . . . very fit to furnish Escrutoires, Cabinets, Corner Cupboards or Sprigs, where chinaware usually stands for Ornament only."[19] From Hampton Court, the insidious charms of "chinamania" had seeped down through the strata of eighteenth-century society, until chinaware became much more than ornament—it symbolized the new way of western life.

With the death of Anne in 1714, England parted with the last of the Stuarts and rode the crest of the wave with the Hanoverian Georges. Even in China, trade was put on a profitable basis when in 1715 the English East India Company was the first foreign trading company permitted a "factory" or warehouse along the swarming quay of Canton. Chinaware could now be ordered to English specifications. The small size of native porcelain tea sets was scarcely adequate for hearty English appetites. Given two years' time, the hill-country potters of Ching-tê Chên, who for centuries had made porcelain for the Emperors of China, now copied tableware of generous western proportions, of five or six hundred matching pieces. Being potters-by-inheritance, they added their own unconscious stamp to every strangely foreign shape they set their hands to. And from the depths of their ancient philosophies, they

---

* *The expression used when a ship successfully anticipated the strong steady wind of the China Sea which blows northward in late summer and autumn and southward in the winter and early spring.*

74) Chinese porcelain covered vase with Fu-dog finial and Ch'i-lin handles.

modeled an occasional knob into a tilted lotus bud or seeded pome-granate or perched a guardian Dog of Fu upon a lid.

As for "embellishing the China," Père d'Entrecolles described the division of painting among many artisans under one roof. "It is the sole Business of one to strike the first colour'd Circle, near the Edges of the Ware; another traces the Flowers, which are painted by a third; it belongs to one to draw Rivers and Mountains, to another Birds and other Animals: as for the Figures of Men, they are commonly the worst done of all."[20]

Louis Le Compte had said the same thing, when he tried to describe the Chinese to his western friends, none of whom had ever seen a Chinaman. "Strangers, who do not know what they are . . . imagine, that they are in effect as monstrous in their shape, as they appear in the Pictures;[21] . . . the Figures that are painted upon the Porcelain Dishes and Cabinets that come from *China*, . . : make them maimed and ridiculous . . . They are not so ill-favoured as they make themselves; . . . they are commonly as Tawny as the *Portuguese* in the *Indies*."[22]

The gossamer brush strokes, mechanically applied by series of youngsters of six or seven years and imitative old men, were picture travel books to the West. In England and on the Continent, fables were spun, books written, plays enacted around them. The whole eighteenth century was enchanted with Charles Lamb by "those little, lawless, azure-tinctured grotesques, that under the notion of men and women, float about, uncircumscribed by any element, in that world before perspective—a china tea-cup."[23] The graceful, swaying *mei jen* of China charmed their way into the hearts of the West and were fondly nicknamed "lange Lyzen" in Holland and "Long Elizas" in England.

To those few who gave any thought to the "china" in the teacup, porcelain remained as much a mystery as ever. Even though in 1727 the French Académie des Sciences published the findings of René de Réaumur of thermometric fame, which he deduced from some clay samples d'Entrecolles had sent him from China, no one but those at Meissen had yet found a supply. Not until 1754 did an English apothecary who dabbled in porcelain discover *kaolin*, and later *petuntse*, in Cornwall. Eventually, by 1765, a deposit was also found in France by a

75) English version of "lange Lyzen" painted in blue on English Lowestoft porcelain. C. 1780.

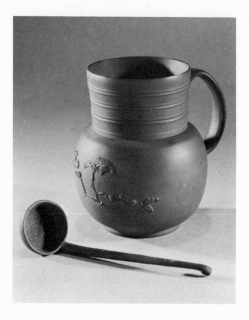

76) A 4-inch-high jug and spoon of unglazed red stoneware attributed to John Dwight of Fulham. English, late 17th century.

chemist. In the meantime, every arcanist developed his own "secret" recipe, adding ground glass, ashes of animal bones, even powdered shards of Chinese porcelain, to the whitest potter's clay he could find, or made "soft" porcelain of soaprock. In the scramble for imitation, a new western art was born.

In Staffordshire, the "red porcelain" of the mysterious Elers brothers tantalized succeeding generations of Midlands potters to persist in their search for a clay that would burn white. Comparative whites—light buff, pale yellow, dingy gray—they molded into teaware shapes like silver or poured into molds to achieve the desired thinness of body, which was believed the only requisite to make their stoneware translucent porcelain. When by chance the temperature of a kiln failed to rise sufficiently to vitrify the refractory material into stoneware, "cream-color ware" resulted. This Josiah Wedgwood perfected to a "useful" ware by 1763. In 1765, he presented Queen Charlotte, wife of George III, with a tea set of his success and received permission to style himself "Potter to the Queen." Wedgwood's fine cream-colored earthenware was now "Queen's ware," but it still wasn't porcelain.

The potteries around cosmopolitan London developed in a more calculated, scientific way. It seems that before the Elers brothers had settled in Staffordshire, they had worked the clays of Fulham on the outskirts

77) Chelsea "Chinaman and Parrot" teapot. English, 1745–50.

of London. As early as 1684 their neighbor there, John Dwight, an Oxford scientist and potter, believed he had solved "the mistery of transparent earthenware comonly knowne by the name of porcelaine or China . . ."[24] and took out a patent to protect his claim. The records show that in 1693 he sued the two Elers and three Wedgwood brothers (ancestors of Josiah) in defense of his "porcelaine" patent rights. Not one of them, however, nor anyone else at that time, had really discovered the secret of the Chinese.

Long after the breach-of-patent suit had been forgotten, porcelain excitement revived again around London. For in 1738, Père du Halde's *Description of the Empire of China* was translated into English, and included were d'Entrecolles's *Lettres Edifiantes* describing "every Branch of the curious Art" of porcelain making as practiced in China. Consequently, quarries and clay pits for miles around were again sifted for deposits comparable to *kaolin* and *petuntse*. As far afield as the "back of Virginia," some was discovered in the early 1740s by one "having read du Halde."[25] And "an earth, the produce of the Cherokee nation in America, called by the natives, *unaker*,"[26] was experimentally imported.

At Chelsea east of Fulham, at Bow, and a half dozen other suburbs, small potteries fanned out from London across the southern half of

78) The china shop of Wedgwood & Byerley in St. James's Square, London, around the close of the 18th century. From R. Ackermann's *Repository of the Arts,* 1809.

England. Each perfected its own secret formula to rival in charm the Chinese. But when the "true" ingredients were finally found in England in 1754, the discovery had lost much of its urgency.

In Queen Anne's day, "the most noble shops in the City [were] taken up with the valuable utensils of the tea-table . . . The china ware-houses were little marts within themselves."[27] That of Pierre Motteux, translator of *Don Quixote,* was "filled and adorned"[28] with "china and japan wares, tea, fans, muslins, pictures, arrack, and other Indian goods."[29] Before long, English-made chinaware gave competition to the East India Company lotteries and candle auctions. By the 1750s, additions of bibelots and home manufactures turned the so-called "china-houses" or "India shops" into "toy" shops stocked with trinkets of fashion and bits of chinaware triumphs of an embryo English industry.

More than one shop must have lured Benjamin Franklin into stealing some minutes from the colonial business that had brought him to London in 1758, for he sent home to Philadelphia "something from all the china works in England." There were "melons and leaves for a desert of fruit or cream, or the like; . . . a Worcester bowl, ordinary . . . [and]

a large fine jug for beer, to stand in the cooler." This, he had fallen in love with "at first sight, for I thought it looked like a fat jolly dame, clean and tidy, with a neat blue and white calico gown on, good natured and lovely, and put me in mind of—somebody,"[30] he coyly wrote his faithful Deborah.

From Bow he chose coffee cups which he packed in the beer jug "in best crystal salt," and also "a bowl remarkable for the neatness of the figures." "Look at [them] with your spectacles on," he wrote Deborah, "they will bear examining." Then "to show the difference in workmanship," he included "one old true china bason mended, of an odd color."[31] It may have reminded him of the first "china" bowl he ever owned, "bought for me without my knowledge by my wife, . . . for which she had no other excuse or apology to make, but that she thought *her* husband deserv'd a silver spoon and China bowl as well as any of his neighbors."[32]

Slowly and modestly the economy of Benjamin Franklin had increased from a frugal "twopenny earthen porringer, with a pewter spoon" to the luxury of "a China bowl, with a spoon of silver."[33] At the same time, the status of his American neighbors had similarly improved to such an extent that in 1765 Josiah Wedgwood declared, "We cannot make anything too rich and costly"[34] for the colonies.

Wares called "White and China ware" had by then already been made in Burlington, New Jersey, "and vended in the Country neighbor plantations and the Islands of Barbadoes Jamaica &C . . . ,"[35] while John Dwight and the Elers brothers still vied with each other at the potteries in Staffordshire. Just as "good porcelain as is made in China" was claimed by Governor Oglethorpe to have been fired in Georgia in 1741 by Andrew Duché—he who had read du Halde and in 1745 was in London peddling his *unaker* from "the back of Virginia." By 1766, Wedgwood was actually "apprehensive" of losing his trade with the colonies, "as they have . . . an agent amongst us hiring a number of our hands for establishing new Pottworks in South Carolina."[36]

However, it was a potter from Bow, Gousse Bonnin, who on December 1, 1769, together with George Anthony Morris of Philadelphia, had "the pleasure to acquaint the public, they have proved to a certainty, that the clays of America are productive of as good Porcelain, as heretofore manufactured at the famous factory in Bow, . . ."[37] It was a "soft"

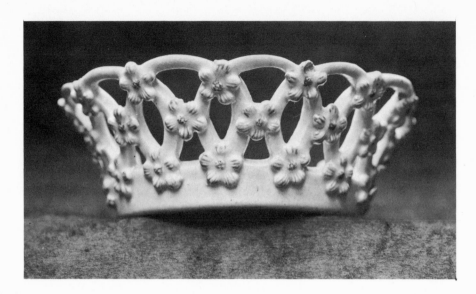

79) Openwork fruit bowl touched with underglaze blue in the flower petals. By Bonnin and Morris of Philadelphia, c. 1770.

80) Blue and white "India china" cup and saucer from one of the many sets used by Martha Washington, both blue and white, and polychrome. From the collection of the James Monroe Law Office Museum.

porcelain of sorts, actually still earthenware. Yet even in their limited success lay their ruin, for England swamped the hungry colonial market with cut-price wares in killing competition. In November 1773, Benjamin Franklin wrote: "the china work in Philadelphia is declined by the first owners. Whether any others will take it up and continue it, I know not."[38] None did for over fifty years.

In the meantime, Charles Willson Peale of Philadelphia advertised during 1795 for "all sorts of fossils, minerals spares, stone, sand, clay, marble, and earthly substances"—for his museum—"from a better knowledge whereof the arts will derive improvement, especially in the manufacturing of Porcelaine, . . ."[39] While at Mount Vernon, Mrs. Washington, for lack of a native porcelain, poured tea into "tiny flaring cups and saucers of blue India China,"[40] ballast now for the China clippers of a young America. As the trade winds steadily blew merchantmen from East to West, the ancient cultures they seeded took root again in new, raw soil.

CHAPTER NINE

In the Chinese Taste

"Of late, 'tis true, quite sick of Rome and Greece,

We fetch our models from the wise Chinese."[1]

—JAMES CAWTHORNE, 1756

CANE and lacquer, cottons, tea and porcelain were those incidentals of trade that made the East tangible to seventeenth-century Englishmen, even while adding confusion to their geography. "India," "China," "Japan" were nothing more than exotic, interchangeable trade names and brought authentic visions to the minds of only those who had sailed the southern seas. All else was fantasy.

China was open a crack to just the Portuguese on Macao, who in one way or another had managed to hold on to their advantage as first arrivals there and had successfully persuaded the Chinese not to permit any other European intruders. In Japan, the Dutch clung to their precarious position in much the same way. As for the English, to the very end of the century, they still could get no closer to China than the treaty port of Amoy or the island of Taiwan, which the Company particularly valued: "that soe if possible by our trading to Tywan it may be in effect as if we did trade to China, Japan and the Manilhaes."[2] In constant search of China goods, they also bartered from the Portuguese at Surat and traded with native junks at Bantam in Java, where the Dutch with their Japan wares likewise broke cargo.

It was a huge, complicated, exciting, uncertain business; but the

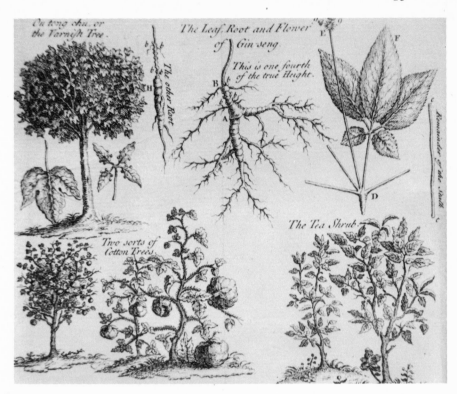

81) "Shrubs and Trees of China." Du Halde selected these as the ones "most likely to raise the Envy of the *Europeans*." Detail from a plate in du Halde's *The General History of China*, 1741.

risks paid off amply in profits to Crown and stockholders. Each time a Company ship piled high its burden on the warehouse wharf in London, Catherine's dowry promise of "a vast Improvement to the *East India Trade*"[3] grew obviously more impressive.

Even so, for reasons private, politic, or financial, some anonymous skeptic publicly doubted in 1676 that the East India trade was "useful to England." On twelve and a half pages of print, the Company answered "The Gentleman": "With a little study and observation he might have learned that it is a trade all nations have and do court at the highest rate [of interest]. A trade the Dutch have adventured their all to purchase; a trade which . . . maintains the Republic in honour, power, and opulency; a trade whereby they have so increased riches and strength as almost to become masters of the world . . . [and] a trade that supplies

82) "Unloading East India Ships at a Wharf Along the Thames." A painting attributed to Samuel Scott (c. 1702–72).

the nation with necessary commodities at a tenth part of the price it must otherwise pay for them. Pepper would be as dear as nutmegs if the Dutch were sole masters of it; calico must be supplied by French, Dutch, and Flanders linen . . ." etc., etc. In case there still remained the slightest doubt, the Company added that the East India trade, "besides giving very considerable customs to the King, brings an annual addition of several 100,000£ to the real stock of the kingdom, and other advantages too numerous to mention . . ."[4]

In the tokens, private trade, and venture cargoes of every India ship that wearily furled its sails at the end of the 15,000-mile run home, the "other advantages too numerous to mention" kept arriving from the East. English homes grew ever brighter, gayer, even cleaner with shiny, colorful, washable goods out of India, China, and Japan. Innovations had been so sudden and extreme since Catherine came to Whitehall that Edmund Waller in his 1683 New Year's tribute to her marveled at

> *What Revolutions in the World have been,*
> *How are we chang'd since we first saw the Queen!*[5]

Certainly then no spotted deer from the forests of India nibbled leaves from the trees in the royal park, nor were there small parrots from Surat in the aviary at Whitehall. The changes were even more noticeable in less royal circles of society, where as early as 1665, Lady Penn (mother of William) showed Pepys "a fine rarity: of fishes kept in a glass of water, that will live so for ever; and finely marked they are, being foreign."[6] From China, actually; there the little gold fish were the playthings of "Princes and great lords," who personally fed them as they rose to the surface of the water at the sound of a clapper.

And from China, too, came the oranges that Pepys first saw grow in an English garden the next year—"some green, some half, some a quarter, and some full ripe, on the same tree; . . . I pulled off a little one by stealth, the man being mightily curious [chary] of them, and eat it, and it was just as other little green small oranges are; . . ."[7] Pepys should more carefully have chosen a ripe one, like the China oranges John Evelyn picked from his own tree in 1679, "as good, I think, as were ever eaten."[8] But then he had never tasted those Catherine had known in Portugal, for even in her youth they were already "Portugal" oranges, thriving there as well as in their native China.

Portugal was but a dream to Catherine in England. While Charles was alive, it was tucked away in some secret crevice of her mind. But after he had died in 1685, it crept back to console her in her abject grief. There was little else left to her, for as Queen Dowager of England, she

83) "Holbein Gate" (c. 1750). A painting by Samuel Scott and Thomas Sandby (1721–98). The Whitehall Banqueting House is at the right. Governor's Office, Palace, Colonial Williamsburg.

was a pawn of power politics, which politely chose to keep her there. Louis XIV's plan was to have James II regain the English throne, and Catherine's presence was necessary to success. In her despair she wrote her brother, Dom Pedro II, King of Portugal: "compliments . . . will not carry me to Portugal, and I have no pleasure nor comfort from being in any other place; . . . I will do my utmost to succeed, for if it depended on me to place myself on a plank, and launch it on the sea, if I had persuaded myself that it would come to Lisbon, I would adventure everything, according to the wish which I have of seeing myself there . . ."[9] Not until 1692, when James failed in his attempt at the Battle of the

Boyne, was she permitted to leave England. Early the next year, when the almond trees were in full bloom around Lisbon, Catherine of Braganza saw again the massive Tower of Belém at the edge of the Tagus, reminder of Portugal's past seagoing glories, and home—where China oranges tasted sweet with southern sunshine, just as she remembered.

In thirty years nothing much had changed at the Portuguese court, not even the farthingales. They made her smile in sad memory of her early days at St. James's. When the ladies of her brother's court asked Catherine to intercede with him for permission to discard their farthingales, she needed all the tact she had acquired in the twenty-three years as wife to Charles II.

Early in 1705, Catherine was unexpectedly appointed Queen Regent of Portugal for her ailing widowed brother. Dom Pedro had lost his

84) The Tower of Belém built on Restello Beach in 1515 to commemorate the sailing of Vasco da Gama from that spot in quest of a maritime route to the East. Originally it stood as a rock in the middle of the Tagus, which since has shifted in such a way that the Tower of Belém is now connected to the land.

Queen when she "dyed with only making A holl in her years for to weare pendants . . ."[10] On the 31st of December, 1705, after less than a year as Queen Regent, Catherine herself died of the colic. She was sixty-seven. For eight days all public business stopped throughout Portugal, all places of amusement remained closed, in as deep respect for Catherine as if she had been Queen in her own right. And for one year, the court of her childhood wore mourning in her memory.

According to her wishes, Catherine was buried in the Mosteiro dos Jerónimos, by the Tower of Belém, the spot from which Vasco da Gama had set sail for the East with the blessing of an earlier sovereign. On his return, the first stone of the Tower was laid in thanksgiving, and the riches of India that subsequently poured into Portugal built more than just a "jewel of architecture." With the burial place of Catherine of Braganza nearby, the Tower became the symbol of an era—an era that ended where it had begun.

Now English ships plowed the oceans to India in the wake of Vasco da Gama's carracks. Trade goods from even China and Japan found devious ways into England, although the Portuguese traders had sat entrenched at the mouth of the Pearl River for almost one hundred and fifty years. By the end of the seventeenth century, the growth of the English East India Company, sped into a burgeoning prosperity by Catherine's dowry gift of Bombay, at long last had tantalized the curiosity and acquisitiveness of the traditionally aloof Emperor of China and had spurred him into action over the protests of the Portuguese on Macao.

K'ang Hsi had been named Emperor by the victorious Manchurians in 1662, the same year that Catherine came to England. Even though conquerors, the Manchus had left undisturbed the Mandarin scholars of the pure Chinese dynasty of Ming, as well as the Jesuit missionaries that had surrounded the court at Peking as astronomers and mathematicians, with all those of lesser rank scattered throughout the interior; for wherever possible, the Manchus adopted the old Chinese culture as they found it. Particularly interested in the crafts of China, K'ang Hsi revived the famous lacquer factory of Peking, rebuilt the fire-demolished porcelain town of Ching-tê Chên, and established no fewer than twenty-seven art-craft worshops in his Peking palace, much as his contemporary Louis XIV of France had done at the Louvre. Then in 1699, on suspicion that there might be gain for China in the foreign trade that

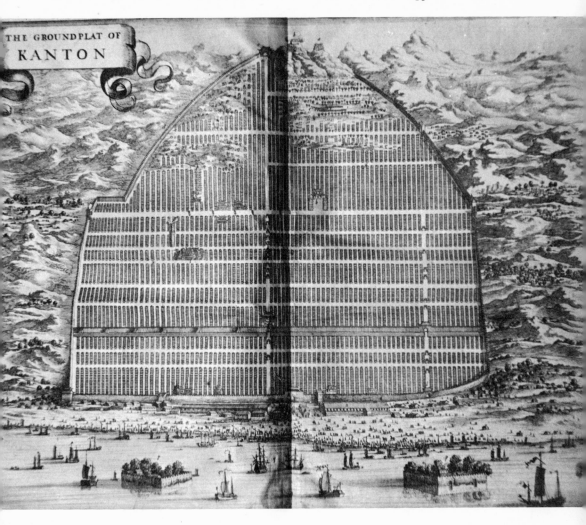

THE GROUNDPLAT OF
KANTON

85) Plat of Canton in 1670, enclosed by its crenellated wall, broken only by the land gate at the top of the plan and two water gates opening to the harbor where Dutch ships ride at anchor between the rectangular "Water Castles." From *An Embassy from the East India Company of the United Provinces,* by John Nieuhoff, "English'd" by John Ogilby, 1673.

had been monopolized for over a century by the Portuguese, K'ang Hsi suddenly opened the port of Canton to the intrepid little English galley, the *Macclesfield.*

China had always spelled enchantment to the English, which years of trade with India had only stimulated, never satisfied. Fed on the

86) A satire on the absurdities of "high-life" fashions, caricaturing hoop skirts and effeminate dandies; monkeys, black servant boys, and "pagods"; exotic menus, cards, and Chinese porcelains. Engraved by Samuel Phillips, 1798, after William Hogarth, 1742.

travel tales circulated ever since the days of Marco Polo to those told by the latest sailor who but briefly set foot on the edge of Chinese soil, generations of young Englishmen had dreamed fantastic dreams of the East when they should have been reading the classics. Even after a century of East India ships tacking their way around the Cape of Good Hope into the Indian Ocean, Cathay was still beyond the next landfall for all but a seasoned few, and Cipangu (Japan) farther still, both gathering allure behind the mists of ignorance. For those at home who drank their China tea from "china" cups, swathed in their China silk or cotton banyans, the "Land of the Dragon Throne" was a very real composite of all their lacquer screens; and Japan, on equally good authority, the place that "had exceeded in beauty and magnificence all the pride of the Vatican at this time and [the] Pantheon before."[11]

Yet when the *Macclesfield* sailed home up the Thames that summer of 1701, "a full and very rich ship," it was her cargo that caused the excitement—not where she had been nor what she had seen. Actually, there were very few in England who seriously cared what China was really like; most people were in love with the land they had spun out of their own imaginations, the idealized creation of their literature and their stage.

King's House, where Pepys spent much of his free time, had been entirely rebuilt after the Great Fire of 1665, "a thousand times better and more glorious than ever heretofore." There "now [were in 1667] wax-candles, and many of them; then [before the fire] not above 3 lbs. of tallow: now, all things civil, no rudeness anywhere; then, as in a bear-garden." Before the fire he remembered there was "nothing but rushes upon the ground, and everything else mean; now, all otherwise; then, the Queen [Catherine] seldom and the King never would come; now, not the King only for state, but all civil people do think they may come as well as any."[12] The new attraction was opera, a revolution in the theater introduced by the Italian musicians Catherine had in her service. "I confess I do admire it," was Pepys's critical comment.

Off and on through the seventeenth century, ever since James I inaugurated "New Yeares night [1604 with] . . . a play of Robin goode-fellow and a maske brought in by a magicien of China,"[13] the theater had been intrigued with this land no playwright had ever seen. With the coming of William and Mary, the love of the exotic took on an even

stronger Chinese flavor. In 1692, Elkanah Settle and Henry Purcell col-
laborated on a musical potpourri called *The Fairy Queen*. The libretto
was based on Shakespeare's *A Midsummer Night's Dream* into which
Settle inserted spectacular pseudo-Chinese diversions such as a ballet
of monkeys and a finale sung against a background of a "transparent
prospect of a Chinese garden" in which "Six pedestals of China-work
rise from under the Stage; [as] support [for] six large vases of Porcelain,
in which are six China Orange-Trees." The music was composed by
Purcell and is still considered probably the most exquisite of his four
operas. The performance was a sensation. Its most exotic innovations
were plagiarized again and again, until in 1755, with Garrick's *Chinese
Festival,* the public had had enough of the Chinese theme. But in the
meantime, monkeys, which had been almost human in *The Fairy Queen,*
now became the badge of high feminine fashion, to the point of satire.[14]

"Mrs. *Trapes* in *Leadenhall* Street is hawling away the Umbrellas for
the walking Gentry, Mrs. *Kanister* . . . buys up all the course Bohee-
Tea . . . , and Mrs. *Furnish* . . . has order'd lots of Fans, and China, and
India Pictures . . . But Madam I ha' . . . the charming'st Monkey for my
Lady that ever was seen; a Coster-monger's wife kiss't it, burst into
Tears, and said, 'Twas so like an only child she had just buried.'"[15]

So buzzed with feminine cupidity the India shops, china marts, and
exchanges in the early years of the eighteenth century. Tea and china,
while still luxuries, were fast becoming staples. But the umbrella, which
had first been noticed in England among Catherine's Portuguese pos·
sessions, was still an "exotic" novelty. Originally built for shade (Latin
umbra) in its native India, the climate of England changed it from a bit
of elegance into a large oiled-silk necessity. Yet as a sunshade, it persisted
as feminine allure.

For the same reason, the 100,000 fans in the holds of the *Macclesfield*
were a shrewd investment. The flat round fans Queen Elizabeth had
carried, had long since been relegated as a fashion "bauble" by Cromwell. Even though Catherine brought the Chinese folding fan with her
from Portugal, it never occurred to her then, modest soul that she was,
that there could be meaning in the whirr, the flip, the snap, the flutter
of the opening and closing tempo of the sticks, nor that the raising or
the lowering of the leaf would speak volumes. But many a foolish
eighteenth-century heart was won or broken by the studied angle of some

87) A shop in Canton filled with an assortment of goods to sell to foreigners. Late 18th century. From a series of 48 ink and wash drawings by an unnamed Chinese artist.

fragile wrist after practiced hours in a fashionable "Fan Academy." Halfway around the world in Canton, to meet the foreign demand, fan makers worked long hours in shops adjoining "the painters upon glass, . . . workers in ivory, japanners, jewellers, and all the various artificers" in New and Old China streets, the only areas "where foreigners might ramble and purchase trinkets."[16]

In the native section of Canton, "Some merchants have several shops in one house, and quite close to one another, in a line," wrote Peter Osbeck in his diary. As supercargo on the Swedish India ship *Prince*

Charles, he found time to wander in and out of the shops that were "quite open towards the street, so that the people that pass by may see every thing" in them. Some houses had as many as five shops, "vaults," opening into each other. However, "The less[er] merchants are satisfied with about two shops, one behind another; in the first of which, . . . is course [sic] porcellane, and in the other all sorts of other wares, as silk, stuffs, hankerchiefs, ribbands, cotton-stuffs, *Indian* ink, painted paper, tea, snuff-boxes made of tutanego, or of copper, with a porcellane enamel, . . . &C."[17]

Then as if by magic, on the days of "great festivals," everything was transformed. "These long, narrow houses are opened, illuminated and ornamented with artificial flowers and trees, which look as if they were the work of nature itself."[18] And from the depths of the last "vault" came the thin, tinny sounds of what passes for music in China.

In the circumscribed commerce of Canton, shopkeepers were allowed to deal only in "lesser" wares; however, porcelain and fashionable trinkets could be decorated to order in the European taste. All other foreign business, from the minute a ship touched Macao, was in the hands of one Chinese official after the other, to the constant irritation, humiliation, and expense of the Europeans. Foreign devils—*Fan Kwaes* —as they were called, were never trusted out of the sight of a responsible Chinaman. They were free only in their choice of the *hong* merchant who would conduct all business for them. From the moment of choice, that official rented them a factory, a *hong,* if they didn't have their own; disposed of their cargo, sold them return goods, all at Chinese prices; and sent them on their protesting way after endless bickerings, evasions, delays, short-dealings, shrewd tradings, and indignities. But they always came back again because in no other place could be had in such variety, and so cheaply, the luxury goods Europe could no longer live without.

From that day in September when the first square-rigger was spotted off the headlands of Macao until the last India ship "saved the monsoon" in January—February at the latest—Canton was a swarming international bazaar. The trade of the world, both East and West, spread along the north beach of the Pearl River from the water's edge to the base of the fortifying wall of the old city. Beyond the wall to the west, the English in 1715 established themselves on the river wharf in a permanent *hong,* flanked by private traders and their native mer-

88) The *hongs* or factories, of Canton, c. 1730. The flags left to right belong to the Dutch, French, English, Swedes, and Danes. Engraved by C. M. Metz (1755–1837). From the *Chater Collection Catalogue,* by James Orange, 1924.

chants. After the English, *hongs* were built there by the French, Danes, Swedes, and Dutch, "each with its national flag flying over it, [in] contrast with the Chinese buildings, and . . . an ornament to the whole."[19] A hundred years later the number had grown to thirteen including both the New England factory and the American.

Picturesque as the waterfront looked to an arriving European, before the first season was over, he knew it as a prison of less than a quarter of a square mile. When the last foreign ship sailed down the river and home, all but the native Cantonese also left. East India Company supercargoes and other resident personnel spent an enforced boredom through the spring and summer on the harbor's outpost of Macao. Only the Jesuit missionaries had access to the interior of China; and it was they who counseled the Company men on matters of custom and protocol, advised them on quality and prices, and shrewdly analyzed the Chinese character.

Du Halde wrote: "They are so full of their own Country, Customs,

Manners, and Maxims, that they cannot be persuaded there is any Thing good out of China." He significantly added: "Honesty is not their favorite Virtue; especially when they have to do with Strangers, whom they seldom fail to cheat, and brag of it."[20] He illustrated his point with several stories, including the one about an English sea captain, which he had obviously borrowed from Père Le Compte. "An English captain having bought some bales of silk of a merchant of Canton: on opening them he found that they were almost all filled with rotten silk; upon which he reproached the Chinese in the severest terms, for his disingenuity and knavery; while the other heard him very unconcernedly, and only made this reply; Blame, Sir, your rogue of an interpreter; for he protested to me, that you would not examine the bales."[21]

Tales such as this were without number, each outstripping the other. But nevertheless, there was profit in the East India trade; some profit, large or small, for each person who touched it anywhere along the way. Samuel Pepys, who had seen its very beginnings, lived now at the turn of the century, in "a very noble and wonderfully well-furnished house, especially with Indian and Chinese curiosities,"[22] according to John Evelyn, who visited him just before Evelyn's eightieth birthday.

Twenty years later, "the present increase of wealth in the city of London" was very obvious to Daniel Defoe, as it "spreads it self into the country, and plants families and fortunes, who in another age will equal the families of the antient gentry, who perhaps were bought out." He counted "above a thousand new foundations [that] have been erected, besides old houses repared, all since the Revolution [of 1688] . . . for such citizens [merchants and tradesmen] as being rich, and having left off trade, live altogether in these neighboring villages, for the pleasure and health of the latter part of their days."[23]

It didn't take long to "equal the families of the antient gentry." The trade that had made the "new rich" continued for decades to pour both wealth and luxuries into England, and no man was modest about his possessions. Pride in possessions was indeed the fashion, to the point of ostentation. In fact, much of the attraction of things from the East was their quality of richness, the contrast of their lush eccentricity with insular English existence.

With the shift of wealth in the population, William Hogarth wrote there was "such a thirst after variety that even paltry imitations of Chinese buildings have a kind of vogue."[24] Horace Walpole actually contended: "The Grecian is only proper for magnificent and public buildings. Columns and all their beautiful ornaments look ridiculous when crowded into a closet or a cheese-cake-house." Then he added, rebel that he was: "I am almost as fond of the *Sharawaggi* or Chinese want of symmetry in buildings as in grounds or gardens."[25]

As early as 1685, Sir William Temple, a friend of both Evelyn and Pepys, had written in his *Essay on Gardening* that the "Chinese scorn" the way the English have of planting their "walks and . . . trees ranged so as to answer one another, and at exact distances . . ." In fact, according to Temple, the Chinese claimed that "a boy, that can tell an hundred," could do as well. On the other hand, their contention was that "the greatest reach of imagination is employed in contriving figures, where the beauty shall be great, and strike the eye, but without any order or disposition of parts that shall be commonly or easily observed."[26] For this, Temple said, "the Chinese have a particular word to express it," which he spelled *sharawadgi*.

"Unshape," Le Compte had called it, for want of a better word for the stylized asymmetrical formality of Chinese art. Never having been subjected to the mathematical rules of the architectural "five orders," China developed a fine sense of unbalance in design that appealed to an England just emerging from circumscribed, classical formality into the unfamiliar comparative freedom of studied naturalness.

English attempts at *sharawadgi* left their mark on the English landscape of parks and architecturally clipped yews, with English interpretations of what the Chinese called "scenes . . . pleasing, horrid and enchanted." This was the way Sir William Chambers expressed the theory of the gardens he had seen around Canton, where, prior to 1755, he had made some limited observations while acting as supercargo for the Swedish East India Company before studying architecture in Paris and Rome. "Enchanted" were those prospects called "romantic" in England, while in "scenes of horror, they [the Chinese] introduce impending rocks, dark caverns, and impetuous cataracts rushing down the mountains from all sides; the trees are ill-formed, and seemingly torn to pieces by the violence of tempests; some are thrown down, . . . appearing as if they had been brought down by the fury of the waters; others look as if shattered and blasted by the force of lightning; . . ."

All this devastation was "generally succeeded by pleasing" scenes, for as Chambers explains, "The Chinese artists . . . [know] how powerfully contrast operates on the mind, . . ."[27]

Even though some seventy years before, Temple had warned against English attempts at Chinese asymmetrical gardening as "adventures of too hard atchievement for any common hands," wagering that "twenty to one they will" fail,[28] yet many a trim row of clipped English evergreens was sacrificed to the rage of "Chinese Taste."

Willows, acacias, camellias, anything that might grow in England, was filched from the soil of China, from as far away as the slopes of the Himalayas, in order to add the currently fashionable naturalism to tortured English landscapes. But at every step, Chinese resistance and guile was encountered, as when Peter Osbeck bought a camellia plant in Canton from "a blind man in the street, which had fine double white and red flowers. But by further observing it in my room, I found that the flowers were taken from another, and one calyx was so neatly fixed in the other with nails of Bamboo, that I scarce have found it out, if the flowers had not begun to wither."[29] In fact, camellias, of the same family as tea, arrived quite accidentally in England as smuggled plants. Westerners had no idea what a tea plant looked like, for they had never seen one grow. Tea and its culture was as deep a Chinese secret as the making of porcelain. Yet time and again, through judiciously placed bribes, some captain or supercargo smuggled out a sprig of a plant that usually shriveled and died long before the Cape of Good Hope was rounded on the long journey home.

Nevertheless, English gardens took on an exotic look by the middle of the eighteenth century. Even when no plan was followed in the planting, there was always a teahouse, often in imitation of a Chinese pagoda with bells hung from the upturned corners of the roof line to frighten away any little devils that might resent the plagiarism. To this day, there still stands a monumental pagoda in Kew Gardens, London, which Chambers built similar to the Porcelain Tower of Nanking, for Augusta, mother of George III. Gone are the eighty gold dragons that protected the corners of the glazed tile roofs, but it still rises nine diminishing stories to its lofty pinnacle, and on a clear day it is said that one can see a distance of forty miles from its top.

Whether built with new money gained in trade or with some properly

89) This "Chinese Pagoda," designed by Sir William Chambers in 1761 for Princess Augusta, mother of George III, still stands today in The Royal Botanical Gardens of Kew, London.

90) Two Chinese gentlemen enjoying a cup of wine while seated on so-called "official's cap" chairs that date back into the Ming period, at least into the mid-15th century. Notice the body-curved back-splat and the cupid's-bow-shaped top rail with "ears" extending beyond the uprights. In cold weather a panel of fur, of quilted fabric or embroidery hangs over the back and seat. From *Sheng yu hsiang chieh (Imperial Edicts)*, with illustrations by Liang Yen-nien, 1681.

inherited, by the 1750s the houses of London and the surrounding counties were "being decorated with china, japan, indian paper, and looking-glasses"[30]—all most probably painted in some little back room in Canton. The "Revolution of Taste" in England had shifted its accent from the "Indian" made available by the dowry of Catherine of Braganza, to that of the now obtainable Chinese. Single objects of value had found their circuitous way from China into England since the days of Elizabeth, but the all-pervading Chinese taste first swept into English living with "Dutch" William and Mary in 1688, when those two were invited to fill the throne left vacant by James II.

Holland with her trading post on Deshima—that spit of artificial land off Nagasaki at the end of Japan, had enjoyed tenuous access to the arts and crafts of China during most of those seventeenth-century years while the English East India Company was struggling to establish itself in India. In that way, long before the English managed more than a trickle of trade in porcelains, the high-shouldered curves of Chinese ceremonial vases suggested the shape for the back-splat on Dutch chairs, and the curve of the vase was also repeated in all four chair legs, after the manner of a Chinese table. But even more obviously, the body-fitting, double curve of the back-splat stems directly from that of Chinese chairs, as does the yoke-shaped cresting rail complete with "ears," later elaborated endlessly by England's Thomas Chippendale. In China, this was but a double-curved version of their "official's cap" chair with its flat toprail and protruding ends, so-called because it supposedly resembled the headdress of sixteenth-century Chinese officials—the narrow-banded brimless caps with stiffly projecting tabs seen pictured in many a Ming porcelain or painting. In fact, it was usually from Chinese porcelains, lacquer-ware, and later from wallpaper that first the Dutch, and then the English, gathered many of their ideas about China and the Chinese way of life and copied what they could.[31]

Possibly even an occasional Chinese book such as the *Imperial Edicts* of 1681, or some earlier historical romance, was carried home as a curiosity by East India Company sailors, either Dutch or English. Only some long-forgotten scholar may have cared about the text, but the wood-block prints, which illustrated the books meant for the general public who could not read, told explicit stories in homey settings that surely excited any English craftsman who turned their folded pages of silky bamboo paper. For the curious, pictures were filled with sensuous foreign ideas of bodily comfort undreamed of by a generation of puritan Englishmen raised on straight-backed, hard-seated chairs and benches. It would not be difficult to believe that among numerous innovations that revolutionized English furniture design in the late seventeenth century, the "long-chair" or "day-bed" had its inspiration in the Ming "drunkard's chair," in which, in the *Edicts,* Tailung of the Han dynasty (so identified by one Chinese authority) is pictured reclining, surrounded by his five industrious daughters.

Just as English artisans after Catherine's arrival adapted the Indian-Portuguese cane and spiral-turnings to English living, so by the end of Queen Anne's short reign in 1714, English craftsmen were still assimilating the Chinese-Dutch ideas that had crossed the Channel with William and Mary. The Anglo-Dutch chairs of the period are today

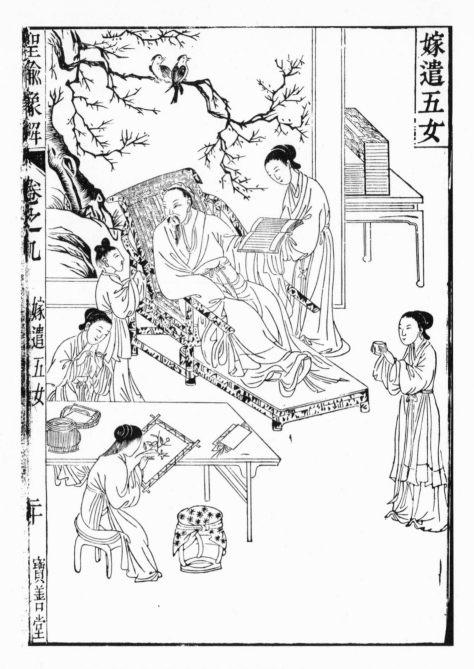

91) A so-called "drunkard's chair" of the Ming dynasty, made of tear bamboo. From *Sheng yu hsiang chieh* (*Imperial Edicts*), with illustrations by Liang Yen-nien, 1681.

called "Queen Anne," with their shaped but unpierced splat, their undulating Chinese curves in cresting, stiles, and legs, and with the spectacular ball-and-claw foot borrowed outright from the Chinese "azure dragon of the East" clutching "the sacred pearl of Buddha." In England, a land of no dragons, nor pearls, it became nationalized into a ball grasped by possibly a hawk's or an eagle's talons.

In the same way, the Chinese bat-of-happiness design served as the back-plate for Queen Anne bale-handled furniture pulls. By the mid-eighteenth century, Chinese cloud-heads dictated the shape of the cutouts that pierced the corner braces in the angle between the straight Chinese legs of Chippendale chairs and the seat. At the same time, endless variations of the Buddhist swastika, or the running key design, or similar Chinese geometric patterns ran down straight chair legs, across aprons and valence boards, and surrounded English tea tables as new-fashioned "fret-work"; while exact English designer-conceived "Chinese lattice" or "paling" was used for banisters, balustrades, and fences.

But it was usually only a bedroom, or more especially its adjoining dressing room in any house of fashionable pretensions, that was completely decorated in the Chinese manner, or as it was still called, "Indian." The one assigned Mrs. Delany at "Cornbury" in 1746, was "hung with the finest Indian paper of flowers and *all sorts of birds* . . . ; the ceilings are all ornamented in the Indian taste, the frames of the glass [mirror] and all the finishing of the room are well suited." As for her bedchamber, that was "also hung with Indian paper on a gold ground, and the bed [was covered with] *Indian* work of silks and gold on white satin."[32]

At "Eastbury" near Salisbury, Mrs. Lybbe Powys of Hardwick House noted in her diary of 1760, that "The *Mangareth,* or Chinese bedroom and dressing-room in the attic storey, is excessively droll and pretty, furnished exactly as in China, the bed of an uncommon size, seven feet wide by six long."[33] It might well have been an exact replica, for beds were occasionally pictured in the Chinese interiors depicted on Ming and Ch'ing dynasty porcelains, screens, and scrolls that found their way into England. Chinese beds were tall, slender, four-post, canopied affairs, functionally much like English ones, except for a low lattice encircling the bed just above the mattress but open for a piece along one long side. William Chambers describes those he saw in Canton, as "of

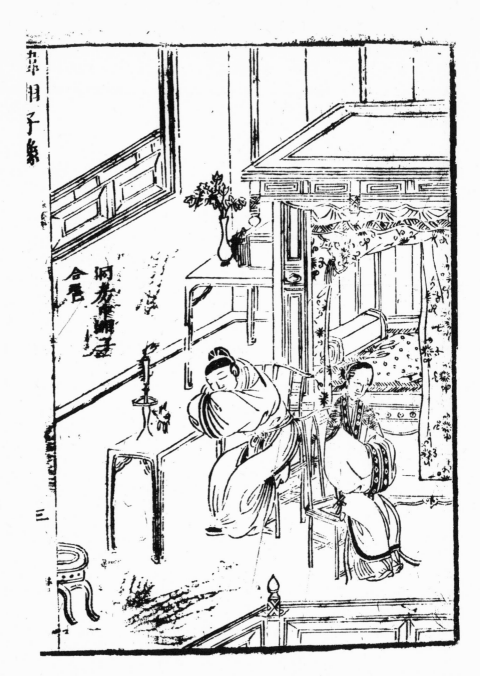

92) A rare view into a Chinese bedroom, c. 1600, that foreshadows English furniture styles of the 1700s. From *Han hsiang tzu chüan* (*The Life of Han Hsiang-tzu*), by Tzu Heng Shan Jên (pseud.), 1623.

rose-wood carved, or lacquered work; the curtains are of taffeta, or gauze; sometimes flowered with gold, and commonly either blue or purple . . ."[34] None of the few that have withstood the ravishes of war, time, and neglect show any of the exaggerated pagoda-roof canopies hung with tassels, or even bells, which Chippendale designed for his English clientele.

Thomas Chippendale borrowed, adapted, and combined from every source available to him; and the results he pictured with explanatory notes in his *Gentleman and Cabinet Maker's Director,* which ran through three editions, starting in 1754. Among the chairs, he drew "Nine Designs of Chairs after the Chinese Manner," which he suggested were "very proper for a Lady's Dressing-Room: especially if it is hung with India Paper."[35] They were lattice-back chairs of differing designs, some with fret-pierced straight legs, all according to Chippendale should "commonly [have] Cane-Bottoms, with loose Cushions; but if required, may have stuffed Seats, and Brass Nails."[36]

And under the heading "China Case" for the display of porcelains acquired during the then prevailing passion of china-mania, he designed several cabinets composed of three or five units of different

93) From Thomas Chippendale's *Gentleman and Cabinet Maker's Director,* 3rd edition, 1762. The armchair was included in Plate XXIII of the 1st and 2nd editions of 1754 and 1755.

94) The comparatively simple "China-case" in the Supper Room of the Governor's Palace, Williamsburg, stands against Chinese wallpaper hand-painted with flowering branches through which flit pairs of all sorts of birds and butterflies. But there is only one owl, for it was said that "Love and Beauty walk hand in hand, but Wisdom walks alone." The pagoda-roof pediment, over the double doors to the Ball Room, continues the Chinese motif, combined in the manner of English carvers, with the Greek fret and acanthus leaf.

size, constructed mainly of glass and lattice doors and panels, with some sections surmounted by bird-cage-like superstructures. To add to the fantasy, each unit of the combination was topped by pagoda roofs of varying styles, but all had up-swept corners, on each point of which hung dripping rococo seaweed, or a tiny bell. Such creations were a world away from the stark simplicity of an actual Chinese interior. But out of the fantastic mixture, which was not alone of Chippendale's making, but was the product of the active imaginations of a whole group of contemporary English artisans with wealthy patrons, evolved the definite English style we now call "Chinese Chippendale."

At the time, as Chippendale himself suggested, certain of these elaborate cabinetmaker's confections were only "very proper" in a room "hung with India Paper." Even though English wallpaper "painters" also produced "Lions leaping from Bough to Bough like cats, Houses in the air, clouds and sky upon the ground, and monsters like the figures in a Chinese paper,"[37] still the imported papers were much preferred, particularly for their exotic colors. Sometimes the color was "the most beautiful pink"—a hot India pink, sometimes a more modest buff, or even a pea green "prettier than 'tis possible to imagine"; but in the dressing room of brilliant Elizabeth Montagu, "Queen of the Blue Stockings,"* "the beauty of colouring . . . [was] carried as high as possible." In her own words, her "dressing room in London is like the Temple of some Indian god: if I was remarkably short and had a great head, I should be afraid people would think I meant myself Divine Honours, but I can so little pretend to the embonpoint of a Josse, it is impossible to suspect me of such presumption." As for the furnishings, "The very curtains are Chinese pictures on gauze, and the chairs the Indian fan sticks with cushions of Japan satin painted."[38]

John Shebbeare could not have been greatly exaggerating when he angrily protested in 1756: "Every chair in an apartment, the frames of glasses and tables must be Chinese: the wall covered with Chinese paper fill'd with figures which resemble nothing in God's creation, and

---

* *Bluestockings were a group of mid-eighteenth-century London ladies and gentlemen who preferred literary conversation to the currently favored cardplaying. It was facetiously named by Boswell, because the botanist Benjamin Stillingfleet, an outstanding conversationalist in the group, was addicted to blue stockings.*

which a prudent nation would prohibit for the sake of pregnant women . . ."[39]

Such a thought never frightened the French, for by the time that England was becoming resigned to the Chinese look, France was already deep in her rococo with a Chinese accent. Because Louis XIV had been as curious about his contemporary, K'ang Hsi, as the Chinese Emperor was about *Le Roi de Soleil*, Louis "resolved [in 1685] to send six Jesuits to China, under the character of his majesty's mathematicians."[40] Louis Le Compte was one of the six that replaced the previous Jesuit advisors to the old Ming dynasty. Through his letters home, and those of the missionaries that followed him into China, the minutest details of Chinese life, arts, and crafts were known first in France.

Le Compte's early letters, starting with his agonizing trip to Peking, formed the basis of du Halde's *Description of the Empire of China*, which stimulated the urge for things Chinese in everyone who could read. The book is still fascinating, for it discusses such Chinese specialties as the raising of tea, gold fish, and "varnish" trees, from which lacquer was made. It comments on the illusiveness of the mythical *Fông-whang*, the Chinese equivalent of the phoenix, and even favorably compares Chinese fashions with the French. But probably most important of all is the fact that from this widely translated work, the secrets of porcelain were ultimately revealed to Europe.

France's early and intimate contact with China had transformed the thoroughly French rococo into an amusing "chinoiserie"—the French idea of Chinese taste. When it crossed the Channel, the style lost a little of its exuberant French temperament in the hands of England's Thomas Chippendale and others of his ilk, but it still showed on occasion, a great flair for the ridiculous. The upturned corners of a pagoda roof were repeated in the cornices of beds and windows, even shaped the exaggerated toprail of some chairs. Monkeys or mandarins scampered through the gnarled branches of candelabras, while the fabulous *Fông-whang* proclaimed his resurrection as proudly as any phoenix from pediment and cresting.

Silver, too, was beaten or cast into similar shapes but suffered aesthetically when forced beyond the simple forms of Chinese porcelain; for silver was foreign to true Chinese living, where porcelain was the most precious material.

Feminine fashions, however, improved with a touch of the Chinese,

95) One of a pair of candlestands with companion girandole, or candle-branches, by Thomas Johnson, a contemporary of Chippendale, whose extravagant designs were often too impractical for execution. C. 1756–8.

96) An English double pagoda-roof silver epergne, with a tiny bell hung on each upturned point. Attributed to Thomas Pitts, 1764.

such as the manner in which Madame de Pompadour combed back her hair with ribbons and flowers tucked into rolled-up tresses. Fifty years before, Le Compte had written from China: "Their Head-dress, . . . interlaced with Flowers of Gold and Silver, is somewhat odd . . . [yet] I am perswaded if People should see the Model of them in *France,* they would go near to be tempted to quit the extravagant Company of Ornaments they use, to dress their Heads à-la-mode de Chineses."[41]

By mid-century, both men and women on each side of the Channel were also wearing "pagoda" sleeves—starched tiers of graduated ruffles for the ladies, and wide out-flaring cuffs for the men, both with the same name. Thirty years later, when a lady's coiffure had risen to a "head" out of reach of her arm, she combed or scratched with a tiny carved hand of ivory or sandalwood at the end of a wand eighteen to twenty inches long, which also came from China.

Nothing escaped the Chinese influence. As *The World* editorialized on March 22, 1753: "According to the present prevailing whim, every thing is Chinese, or in the Chinese taste; or, as it is sometimes more modestly expressed, *partly after the Chinese manner*. Chairs, tables,

97) Pagoda-like tea alcove in the Chinese room at "Claydon House," decorated by the second Earl Verney, c. 1765, when he enlarged the ancestral home where Mary Verney, his step-aunt, had been a child—she who asked her father's permission to learn to "Jappan" around 1690, when that art was very new to England. The carving here is entirely of wood, even to the tiny bells that hang from the eaves; and the bamboo furniture is of the period, the kind made in Canton by the Chinese for export.

chimney-pieces, frames for looking-glasses, and even our most vulgar
utensils, are all reduced to this new-fangled standard; and without
doors so universally has it spread, that every gate to a cow-yard is in T's
and Z's, and every hovel for the cows has bells hanging at the corners."[42]
Three years later, John Shebbeare moaned: "Nay, so excessive is the
love of Chinese architecture become, that at present the fox-hunters
would be sorry to break a leg in pursuing their sport in leaping any gate
that was not made in the eastern taste of little bits of wood standing in
all directions, . . ."[43]

"The scope and variety which it afforded" endeared the Chinese
taste to eighteenth-century imaginations. In the hands of an amateur,
it was often nothing more than a shoddy combination of "a good choice
of chains and bells, and different colours of paint. As to the serpents,
dragons, and monkeys, etc., they, like the rest of the beauties, may be cut
in paper and pasted on anywhere, or in any manner."[44] But for those
with finer sensibilities and more money, taste for the Chinese expressed
itself in a "back-painting" on glass, or on looking glass, done for miserable pay and much profit in Canton; or in a ball gown, a gentleman's
waistcoat, or such, stamped in England and embroidered in China
with closely laid stitches of floss silk, or even painted; but most probably
it showed in a tea set, or a dinner service of several hundred pieces
painted to order at Canton with crest or cipher to celebrate the knight-
ing of a gentleman or his wedding.

Porcelain painted in Canton "according to particular directions, or
with names, or coat of arms, is very dear,"[45] even by the standards of the
1750s, and was not for every Englishman. However, those with a desire
for the Chinese could achieve a satisfactory effect with English-made
imitations of the real thing. Elizabeth Montagu suggested to a friend
that "she might furnish . . . in the present fashion, of some cheap paper
and ornaments of Chelsea China or the manufacture of Bow, which
makes a room look neat and finished." But she added, "They are not
so sumptuous as mighty Pagodas of China or nodding Mandarins."[46]

Chinaware factories sprang up all over England; many failed in the
face of competition from the preferred Chinese porcelains. Others only
survived by deliberately filching Chinese designs, such as the old stere-
otyped Chinese landscape combination of rocks balanced by the con-

98) English blue "willow pattern" plate with an openwork border. Early 19th century.

trasted foliage of a willow tree and a pine, with stylized clouds floating over all.

In 1780, young Thomas Minton, while an apprentice at the Caughley Pottery Works, designed a pseudo-Chinese fantasy on this pure Chinese prototype, and with imagination assembled the ingredients of a love story on English dinner plates. The first year the design was hand-painted in traditional Chinese cobalt blue; thereafter it was transfer-printed in quantities. But almost from the beginning, a charming tale was spun around the three little figures on the humpback bridge in the foreground, and somehow the transplanted ancient pine now bore rows of English apples, while a pair of doves fluttered in the sky where once Chinese clouds serenely floated.

Koong-see was the name of the young girl fleeing across the bridge with her lover, both pursued by her irate Mandarin father close behind. Koong-see once lived in that pagoda-roofed house between the exotic pine and willow trees, protected by the fence of Chinese "paling," at the side of the lake or stream across which she now fled. But she had fallen in love with her father's secretary, Chang—even while her father had plans to "marry her off to some wealthy Ta-jin, as soon as the peaches to blossom begin." The story goes that Chang rescued her on her wedding day and fled with her over the timeless humpback bridge—

Koong-see carrying her distaff, Chang a salvaged jewel case, both chased by her angry father, whip in hand. In true fairy-tale fashion, the two lovers escaped in a junk and sailed away to live in their tiny cottage at the top of the plate until discovered by the "wealthy Ta-jin," who burned their little love nest down about their ears. From the heap of ashes, benevolent gods then changed the young lovers into a pair of twirling turtle doves that have ever since dominated the center of the "Willow Pattern."[47]

The combination of charming design and poignant story carried this bit of "Chinese Taste" into every English home and across the Atlantic ever since its origin in 1780. Not only did other English potters copy it, but Chinese merchants in both Nanking and Canton, sure of a ready market, made the pattern their own—a tacit admission that English china was now serious competition to Chinese porcelain.

In fact, England attempted to manufacture anything fashion took to its heart, whether made in China, or in India for that matter. It was even stated on good authority at the time that "not one in a thousand of all the stiles, grates, rails, pales, chairs, temples, chimney-pieces, &c. &c. &c. which are called Chinese, has the least resemblance to any thing that China ever saw; . . . [because] . . . our Chinese ornaments are not only of our own manufacture, like our French silks, and our French wines; but, what has seldom been attributed to the English, of our own invention."[48] Small wonder that every traveler through England remarked on the country's prosperity: "Take notice of the spirit with which manufactures are carried on . . . Move your eye which side you will, you behold nothing but great riches and yet greater resources . . ."[49]

More than any one thing, the Company men who returned to England oozed this prosperity and personified in themselves the successful trade of a century and a half in the East. Sent out as apprentices to "writers"* at fourteen or so, these sons of merchants, of impoverished nobility, or of Company directors, returned home after a lifetime in the tropics with much more than recipes for curry and punch, and their native house boys. They were trained to demand, accustomed to be served, and were flamboyantly ostentatious with mysterious wealth. All

* Apprentices of seven years became "writers" in the Company. After writers had served their time, they were "factors"; and after some more years they were called "merchants," then "senior merchants."

99) A returning "Nabob" distributing India's riches to expectant Englishmen, ranging from the prostrate Queen and her scraping consort to the assorted classes of men as designated by the hats in their outstretched hands. By James Gilray, 1788.

this combined to dub them "Nabob," the anglicized version of *Nawab*, a minor Mohammedan government official. England had grown rich on their exile, on their risks and business acumen. Smug stay-at-homes shunned, yet secretly envied these returned "Asiatic Grandees," these "Mushroom Gentlemen," for their too obvious, transplanted, exotic splendor; but most especially, for their personal success in the odious world of trade. Yet in their very success, Nabobs symbolized Daniel Defoe's premise of 1728: "Trade nourishes Industry, Industry begets Trade; . . . Trade is the Wealth of the World."[50]

That was the vision Edward Hyde had held for England when he urged Charles II to take Catherine of Braganza as his Queen, because, as he reasoned, the benefits to trade contained in the treaty "might reasonably be valued above the Portion in Money."[51] It was to defend

100) The parlor of the Palace at Colonial Williamsburg with the japanned twelve-scallop pedestal tea table set for tea, the galleried kettle stand at hand for the hostess in the Chinese Chippendale armchair, which is carved with temple bells and has coolie-hat ears terminating its top rail.

the trade that had been coaxed out of Catherine's dowry that England found herself fighting on three continents and the ocean lanes between for much of the last quarter of the eighteenth century. In the words of the Earl of Sandwich: "We have no one friend or ally [in 1779] . . . all those who ought to be our allies except Portugal, act against us."[52]

Like others grown used to luxury, Horace Walpole wished for "time to lay in a stock of tea and sugar for the rest of one's days." For as he wrote the Countess of Upper Ossory on November 14, 1779: "I think only of the necessaries of life, and do not care a rush for gold and diamonds, and the pleasure of stealing logwood. The friends of Government [with whom he was out of sympathy], who have thought of nothing but of reducing us to our islandhood, and bringing us back to the simplicity of ancient times, when we were the frugal, temperate, virtuous old English, ask how we did before tea and sugar were known."[53]

There were actually few who could remember for themselves, but their fathers would have known. For in but one quick century, tea and sugar became "the necessaries of life"; washable porcelain and cottons had contributed to a dramatically reduced death rate; and the government found itself with half of Asia on its hands in order to preserve the fabulous trade that had built eighteenth-century England into an Empire.

CHAPTER TEN

The Completion of the Circle

"The Arts have always travelled westward, and there is no doubt of their flourishing hereafter on our side of the Atlantic."

— BENJAMIN FRANKLIN

THE same year in which Vasco da Gama pioneered the sea route to the Indies around the tip of Africa, 1497, John Cabot persuaded England's Henry VII that the way to the East lay west. Even though Cabot was back in England in three months with but a holdful of fat cod, he had sighted land through the fog of the Grand Banks off Newfoundland. For this, this Genoese sailor from a Levant spice ship received £10 from the English king, recorded as a gift "to hym that found the new Isle."[1]

The fever of exploration in the early sixteenth century touched every land within smell of the sea. Spain pushed deeper into the riches of new conquests—even to the Philippines—as far as she dared go toward the East. By 1566 she found it necessary to build a fort at St. Augustine, Florida, as safe harbor from sea rovers for her highly tempting treasure fleets. France, too, joined in the search for the water route of Columbus westward to Cathay and Cipangu, and sent Verrazano, then Cartier, to probe the coast of America for through passage to the East. Finally, in 1576, Henry VII's granddaughter, Elizabeth I, entered the competition, first sending Sir Martin Frobisher across the Atlantic to find a shortcut through America, then the luckless Sir Humphrey Gilbert, followed by a series of ventures sponsored by his half brother, Sir Walter Raleigh. At the end of December of 1600, disappointed in the results of these exploits, Elizabeth chartered the Governour and Merchants of London Trading into the East Indies, committed to follow the Portuguese around the Cape of Good Hope.

The Dutch East India Company, however, even while using the conventional route around Africa to her holdings in the Spice Islands, employed the Englishman Henry Hudson in 1609 to sail west across the Atlantic to search out the Northwest Passage through the great American obstruction—a passage everyone knew must be there. In the *Half Moon,* Hudson sailed miles up the river that was to bear his name, before he was convinced it led to no sultry Spice Islands. Only furs, the

101) A 1577 map of Virginia, from New England to Florida and west to "The Sea of China and the Indies." The legend confirms the belief that the "proffitable rivers . . . necessarily must run into y^t peacefull Indian Sea. . . ."

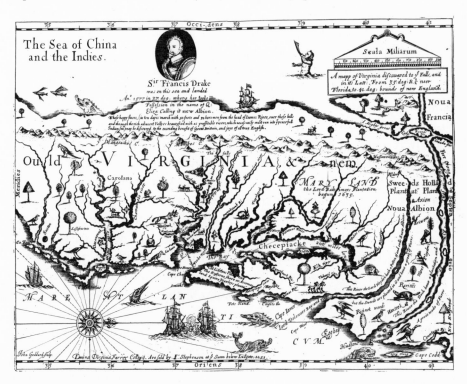

thick pelts of otter and beaver, were offered in trade by the Indians. On that trade, at the point on the river where Hudson turned back, was founded Fort Orange, now Albany, in 1624; and two years later Fort Amsterdam was established on the southern tip of Manhattan Island as a base for the Dutch West India Company, newly formed for privateering against the Spanish in the Caribbean.

From the first, the Dutch Colony of New Netherlands flourished as a trading post for the four corners of the world. By the mid-seventeenth century, the skin of a "good whole beaver" brought eight to ten seventeenth-century guilders at Fort Orange; and at Fort Amsterdam those not engaged in the fur trade got rich on smuggling and privateering. As was said of their cousins in Holland: "They keep their houses cleaner than their bodies, and their bodies cleaner than their souls."[2] The deep-living New World burghers lacked nothing their friends and relations across the Atlantic valued.

As in old Amsterdam so in Dutch America, a great cupboard or *Kast* on enormous ball feet dominated every room in the house, often with a *Knopf* at each corner of the wide cornice, as "guardians of the porcelain ornaments which decorated the top."[3] Of porcelain, "real" Chinese or delft, there was never a shortage. "They set out their cabinets and bouffetts much with china . . . [and] hang earthen or delft plates all round the walls in manner of pictures, having a hole drilled thro the edge of the plate or dish and a loop of ribbon put into it to hang it by."[4] Flower pots, cisterns, basins, and plates; porcelain tea dishes, tea cups, tea saucers, and numerous small red or white teapots; and always "small images" of men, dogs, swans, ducks, lions filled their houses and later pages of inventory of their estates—valued in English pounds, or in two and three times as many beaver skins.

The term "East India" qualified boxes of silver, ebony trays, "varnished" cabinets, which the English called "japanned," and dozens of pictures in red "lists," or frames. As for fabrics, the table carpets and curtains of calico and chintz, the quantities of waistcoats, stomachers, aprons, nightcaps, and "nightgowns" of calico only emphasized the pervasive power of fashion and the extent of the East India trade, legitimate and otherwise, even in America.

Off and on throughout the seventeenth century, there was war between England and Holland, fought especially in areas of the world where their trade conflicted. In Asian waters, the Spice Islands had been the rich stake of contention ever since the rival East India companies had intruded into the Portuguese monopoly. While in the New World, several ships of Charles II's fleet sailed unannounced into New Amsterdam harbor on the twenty-ninth of August, 1664 (old style), and laid claim to New Netherlands, as part of the territory John Cabot had discovered for England. "Without a blow or a tear," the Duke of York was richer that day by a grant of land that extended from the Connecticut River to the Delaware. When the Peace of Breda was signed in 1667, the price England paid for New York was to forfeit all claims to the Spice Islands—those bits of fragrant, exotic allure, in search of which Henry Hudson had sailed up his river, and which, yet earlier, had actually instigated the discovery of America in the first place.

As for the bustling sailor's town of New Amsterdam, rechristened New York, the English had grasped a pirates' nest. Privateering was the legitimate game of taking an enemy merchant ship as a prize of war. Smuggling was the dangerous sport of outwitting the government of customs due. But piracy was plundering with violence on the high seas, and even in those vicious times was regarded with contempt. That is, officially; the spirit behind these definitions changed with each situation.

While it was still New Amsterdam, a report of 1654 made to the Director General of the Dutch West India Company, stated that "pirates and vagabonds are countenanced, favoured, harboured, entertained, and supported by subjects and inhabitants having fixed domicile . . ."[5] Practically every little cove along the East River sheltered some pirate ship, most of them English. Forty years later, such swashbuckling captains as Shelly, Tew, and the controversial Kidd, still called New York "home," as did many others who operated around Madagascar off the east coast of Africa in the Indian Ocean.

" 'Tis the most beneficiall trade[,] that to Madagascar with the pirates[,] that was ever heard of," wrote the Earl of Bellomont to the Lords of Trade in London, "and I believe there's more got that way than by turning pirates and robbing."[6] Law-abiding merchants, Dutch and otherwise, saw no crime in pleasing their customers with pirated East India goods, and lining their pockets in the bargain. They felt "it as a violence done them" when the government seized "unlawful goods in their warehouses and shops."[7]

After fifty years of indulgent or corrupt regimes, both Dutch and

102) The Swaggering Pirate, Captain Bartho. Roberts, with his ships flying the black flags of his profession. From Charles Johnson's *A General History of the Pyrates, from Their First Rise and Settlement in the Island of Providence, to the Present Time,* 1725. It is supposed that Daniel Defoe was the actual author.

English, the Earl of Bellomont was appointed royal governor in 1698, especially instructed to suppress piracy. In reporting his progress to London, he wrote: " 'Tis almost incredible what a vast quantity of East India goods would have been brought into this port had there not been a change in the Government." In fact, he went on to say, there had been eight or nine pirate ships at "the mouth of this port . . . since my coming . . . and by the confession of the merchants in the town they would have brought in a £100,000 in gold and silver, and this inrages them to the last degree that they have missed of all this treasure and rich pennyworths of East India goods . . ."[8]

It is a matter of conjecture just where those bales of silks and calicoes, those chests of porcelain, possibly even of tea, were auctioned off. Next to New York, New England was considered a very likely market for plundered goods. The Puritans themselves condoned smuggling. As for piracy, just two years before, the notorious Captain John Avery, he with a Mogul's daughter as wife in Madagascar, had readily disposed of his questionable cargo in Boston. Pirates were as welcome there as in New York, for besides supplying New Englanders with the exotic luxuries which were becoming as necessary to them as to England, "pirate's gold" lubricated the channels of trade.

In many of the colonies, very little money actually changed hands in a legitimate transaction; it was usually just a matter of bookkeeping, or barter. But pirates paid in Spanish doubloons, in Portuguese crusadoes, or in the raw mined wealth of unmapped places. After Captain Kidd was hanged, however, in May of 1701, piracy along the eastern seacoast fell on cautious days, and the flow of East India goods temporarily slowed into New York and the harbors of New England.

As early as 1663, the Boston "Merchants and such as are increasing cent per cent"[9] were warned by their Puritan clergy to remember that New England was "originally a plantation of Religion, not a plantation of Trade."[10] Nevertheless, a doctrine that related an honest man's worldly success to his obvious favor in the sight of God quite naturally brought about an accumulation of material wealth.

Such was the faith that rewarded Boston-born Elihu Yale with an estate he estimated in 1691 at "above five hundred thousand pagodas" —some $5,000,000 at that time—after "twenty years diligent Service in India and Tradeing" for the East India Company. This was before the days when obvious East India riches labeled an Englishman "Nabob." However, the astounding fact of such fabulous wealth acquired by one who quite accidentally had spent the first three years of his life in New England marked him for posterity. Some twenty-seven years later, shrewd Cotton Mather flattered the aging expatriate in London by writing on February 14, 1718: "There are those in these parts of western *India,* who have had the satisfaction to know something of what you have done and gained in the *eastern,* and they take delight in the story . . ."[11]

To pry loose some of these gains for the struggling "Collegiate School" of Connecticut, Mather suggested to Elihu Yale that "if what is forming at New Haven might wear the name of YALE COLLEGE, it would be better than *a name of sons and daughters.* And your munificence might

103) The earliest view of Yale College after its removal to New Haven in 1717, when it was first called "Yale." After a drawing by John Greenwood.

easily obtain for you such a commemoration and perpetuation of your valuable name, which would indeed be much better than an Egyptian pyramid."[12]

That June, Elihu Yale responded with a three-part gift consisting of a portrait of the reigning sovereign, George I, turned out by the fashionable painting mill of Godfrey Kneller, which still hangs at Yale; two "trunks of textiles"—quite probably East India textiles Yale had collected during his years of service to the Company, which he stipulated were "to be sold or otherwise Improved for the Benefitt of the Collegiate School in New Haven"; and four hundred seventeen books, two hundred and sixty-two titles of which are still on the shelves of Yale University. In addition, he willed a "munificence" of £500 "To Connecticote College," the "Collegiate School" in New Haven. After Yale's death, his estate took forty days to sell at auction, but not one penny of that promised legacy of £500 ever reached the school, which nevertheless changed its name to Yale College.

Even though Yale was the only American "Nabob" of record, tangible wealth to the point of luxury seeped all through New England. By 1700, "a Gentleman from *London* would almost think himself at home at *Boston,* when he observes the Numbers of People, their Houses, their Furniture, their Tables, their Dress and Conversation, which perhaps is as splendid and showy, as that of the most considerable Tradesman in *London.*"[13]

To the surprise of more than one traveler of the day, "there is no Fashion in *London,* but in three or four Months is to be seen at *Boston.*"[14] Samuel Sewall drank tea as casually as any Englishman by 1709; and in 1712 he regretted the loss of the "Japanner" who had worked in Boston. But "a True Looking Glass of black Walnut Frame of the newest Fashion (if the Fashion be good)"[15] he had to order from London, together with cane chairs by the dozen; and in the spring of 1724, he dressed his third wife in a "new Gown of Sprig'd Persian"—a thin China silk—that could not be had in Boston.

In long-distance ordering, much had to be left to chance or the good taste of the Merchant in London. Yet those who knew what they wanted sent minute instructions, as Thomas Hancock (uncle of John), who ordered "paper-hangings" painted in the "Chinese Taste," after a remnant he sent over as a sample. He described them as having "In other parts of these Hangings . . . Great Variety of Different Sorts of Birds, Peacocks, Macoys, Squirril, Monkys, Fruit and Flowers, etc.," and suggested that "if they can make it more Beautifull by adding more Birds flying here and there, with some Landskips at the Bottom, Should/ like it well." Even though he wanted to outshine his neighbors, yet his native thrift prevailed to add, "by all means . . . get mine well Done and as Cheap as Possible."[16]

While the English East India Company made "Chinese" the rage in England, little found its way directly from Asia into the colonies; and no ship, English nor colonial, dared trespass on the far eastern monopoly of the Company, as the *Eugene* learned to her sorrow. Rich from "slaving" on the coast of Madagascar, she had been forced by pirates there—"who lie in wait for the East India Men"—to equip them with men and provisions in return for "some valuable Presents of Money, &c." According to the account in the *American Weekly Mercury* of August 3, 1721, her captain, upon reaching Virginia, was unceremoniously placed on an English man-of-war "to be carried Home for his Tryal, not for any Dealings with the Pyrates, but for having on Board East India Goods."

England's economic policy of national self-sufficiency began as early as 1660 to lay a heavy hand on her colonies. Foreign goods must first be "laid on the shores of England" before being transhipped to the colonies, with consequent multiplication of costs and customs. Only ships built, owned, and manned by Englishmen or English colonials could carry trade between them. These were the *Acts of Trade and Navigation* that were flouted and circumvented with flagrant brazenness from the coast of Maine to Chesapeake Bay.

New Englanders, frustrated by their rocky soil, turned to building sloops, snows, brigantines, for fishing and trade-carrying, coastwise and to the West Indies, eventually even across the Atlantic. By the turn of the eighteenth century, ship carpenters, joiners, or the more skillful cabinet makers made for all but their most fashionable neighbors tall, narrow-backed chairs called "banister-backs" by substituting vertical flat spindles for India cane. Black paint changed turned split-spindles and egg-shaped bosses into fashionable "ebony" decorations on local court cupboards, or simulated Chinese lacquer on a chest of pine. By the

104) New England court cupboard of oak decorated with bosses and split-spindles. Andover, Massachusetts, dated 1684.

105) New England japanned high chest-of-drawers with a Bactrian camel among assorted exotic birds and pseudo-Chinese figures slightly raised. The steps are original with the piece, made expressly for the purpose of exhibiting the precious salt glaze and delft of the period, and Chinese porcelains when available. C. 1700.

beginning of the eighteenth century, New England was practically self-sufficient in the crafts and actually was shipping furniture made from her own trees to planters around Chesapeake Bay.

Virginians, on the other hand, had found their fortunes not in trade alone, nor in farming, but in the grandiose combination of the two. After almost a century of dramatic failures and back-breaking fresh starts, the fittest among them had built a dominion of tobacco plantations out of their own headrights and those of their indentured white servants—each headright being fifty acres of free land for each paid passage to Virginia. With tobacco, the money that grew broad-leafed and green right out of their own rich, black bottom lands, they furnished the houses they built along the estuaries of Virginia's four great rivers and on the banks of a number of lesser ones, all "navigable for vessels of great burthen." On their docks and landing places "any thing may be delivered to a gentleman there from London, Bristol, etc., with less trouble and cost, than to one living five miles in the country in England."[17] In fact Robert Beverley, one of their own number, accused them as "abominable Ill-husbands, that tho' their Country be over-run with Wood, yet they have all their Wooden Ware from *England;* their

Cabinets, Chairs, Tables, Stools, Chests, Boxes, Cart-Wheels, and all other things, even so much as their Bowls, and Birchen Brooms."[18]

With the development of the triangular molasses-rum-slave trade in the eighteenth century, Negro slaves became the servants of the South. "Several of them are taught to be sawyers, carpenters, smiths, coopers, etc. . . . though for the most part they be none of the aptest or nicest."[19] Craftsmen of any kind continued scarce and indifferent. Not only "Wooden Ware" was shipped from London in empty tobacco ships, but medicines, hardware, exotic foods, sundries, and notions filled pages of shipping invoices.

Clothes and furnishings proved the greatest gamble in cross-ocean shopping. In 1760, George Washington minced no words to Robert Cary, merchant of London. "It is needless for me to particularize the sorts, qualities, or taste I would choose to have them in, unless it is observed; and you may believe me when I tell you, that, instead of getting things good and fashionable in their several kinds, we often have articles sent us, that could only have been used by our forefathers in days of yore."[20]

"Fashionable" had always been that quality in anything that made a transplanted Englishman feel himself not so far from London. Consequently, it was no accident that Virginians, even in the first quarter of the eighteenth century, "live in the same neat manner, dress after the same modes, and behave themselves exactly as the gentry in London."[21] Only pets were different in Virginia, as William Byrd found out when in 1728 he called on Mrs. Spotswood, the ex-governor's lady. For "amongst other favorite animals that cheered this lady's solitude, a brace of tame deer ran familiarly about the house." A few minutes after Byrd had been ushered "into a room elegantly set off with pier glasses," one of the deer, "spying his own figure in the glass . . . made a spring over the tea table that stood under it . . . shattered the glass to pieces, and falling back upon the tea table made a terrible fracas among the china."[22] But even in ruins, the room was "fashionable" by any standards.

Much the same flair for rich living, but polished into a suave urbanity, marked the city of Charles Town in South Carolina. Built from the start on a merchant-planter hierarchy of wealth supported by slaves, its mixture of Restoration Royalists with French Huguenots and some plantation owners from the Barbadoes, gave the city a colorful air of "Asiatic splendour." "Fine laces of Flanders, the finest Dutch linnens, and French cambric, chintz, Hyson Tea, and other East India goods, silk, gold, and silver laces, etc."[23] were annually imported into the city, according to Governor Glen. While outside the harbor, up and down the coast, lurked privateers turned pirates, or true professionals like Captain Teach called "Bluebeard," to bully a share of the rich trade, coming and going. Rice was the staple, grown from seeds not long out of Madagascar; and in the 1740s, the profits from indigo raised another group of millionaires. Even as their counterparts in the other colonies, Charlestonians "in proportion as they thrive . . . delight to have good things from England."[24] By 1760, Charles Town was the fourth city in the colonies, Philadelphia the largest.

Philadelphia, in fact, was then second in size only to London in the whole British Empire. Charles II never would have dreamed it when in 1681 he chartered a good-sized slice of the Duke of York's New Netherlands grant to the Quaker son of his old-time benefactor, Admiral Penn. William Penn had not always been a Quaker. Samuel Pepys first met him as a young cavalier just returned from Paris in 1664. "I perceive something of learning he hath got, but a great deal, if not too much, of the vanity of the French garb, and affected manner of speech and gait."[25] In eighteen years much of that youthful "vanity" had worn off, but his love of fine things Penn carried with him into the New World.

More important to his "Holy Experiment" were his faith in humanity and ideas on religious freedom, added to the Quaker precept that all be "Kept employed in some lawful calling, that they may be diligent, serving the Lord in the things that are good; that none may live idle, and be destroyers of the creation. . . ."[26] The combination spelled success for the colony from the beginning. Even though the percentage of Quakers was scarcely a third, the atmosphere they created—serene, industrious, substantial—molded the character of the whole city.

By 1775, with 20,000 citizens, Philadelphia had already passed New York and Boston in size, its houses "all of brick; . . . a pent* over the base storey, and shops, and a little slip of a window to light a closet by the

---

* *A pent is an eave that projects from a house wall at the height of the first story. Originally designed to protect half-timbered walls from the elements.*

side of the chimnies. . . ."[27] Farther out along the two rivers, and in the valleys in between, were scattered little week-end "plantation" houses and the grander country seats of many of the same Quaker merchants who owned those prim brick houses in town.

Behind sober façades, usually could be found an example or two of the newest English fashion in the "Chinese Taste." As merchants, fashion was good business; as sea captains and ship owners, the fashion for things from the East had the added appeal of forbidden fruit. For stay-at-home travelers, Stalker's *Treatise of Japanning and Varnishing* opened exciting pseudo-Chinese vistas, here as in England. Before mid-century, lacquer-ware could be ordered in both Boston and New York from an occasional craftsman who "hereby gives Notice, that he Makes [among other] things all Sorts of Japan-Work, of divers fine Colours, to that Degree, that none heretofore hathever exceeded him in that Art."[28] Merchants with connections in London sent directly for "raised Japan'd Black Corner cubbards"—those from Philadelphia with conservative Quaker taste, stipulating "no Red in 'em, of the best Sort, but Plain."[29]

Real porcelain, or delft imitations of the real thing, crowded colonial shelves; and tea dishes were set out on "new-fashioned" mahogany tea tables, dominated by the sheen of silver vessels beaten out of a percentage of the foreign coinage that circulated in every seaport town. Tea, in fact, even at 28s. a pound, had become just as popular in the colonies as it was in England. Dr. Alexander Hamilton of Annapolis, who in 1744 traveled on horseback as far as Maine, up to Albany and back, wrote in his diary that he had even been served "an elegant dish of scandal to relish"[30] his tea. But Ann Whitall, a sensitive Quakeress, confided to her diary: ". . . O I think my eyes could run down with tears always for the abomination of the times! So much excess of tobacco; and tea is as bad, so much of it, and they will pretend they can't go without it. And there is the calico! Oh the calico! I think tobacco and tea and calico may all be set down [together], one as bad as the other."[31]

Two hundred chests of tea a year were imported by Philadelphia merchants in the 1750s, over half of which were smuggled in from the Dutch. To the housewife it was all the same; even to Deborah Franklin, who spread her tea table with the breakfast cloths her husband sent her from London, "for nobody breakfasts here on the naked table, but

106) Susanna Truax, a little four-year-old American girl, putting sugar into a "dish" of tea on an
American tea table. Painted by an unknown artist
in March 1730.

on a cloth they set a large tea-board with the cups."[32] Little did he
realize then the significant role tea was to play in the next ten years.

In March 1765, the fateful Stamp Act was passed, and the "Non-
Importation" answer from the colonies followed immediately after.
Within months English manufacturers felt its impact. "A ship actually
returned from Boston to Bristol [England] with nails and glass," wrote
Franklin in deep satisfaction, "and ships . . . are actually returning to
North America in their ballast."[33]

After a century of Acts of Parliament designed to keep the colonies
indefinitely dependent on English manufacturers, Englishmen found it
difficult to believe that their colonies in the midst of a wilderness could
possibly do without their merchandise, could even exist without English

wool, their traditionally pampered trade. Quite seriously a newspaper stated that American sheep grew only wool "sufficient for a pair of stockings a year to each inhabitant." To which Franklin facetiously replied that the very tails of the sheep "are so laden with wool, that each has a little car or wagon on four little wheels, to support and keep it from trailing on the ground." "Perhaps," he added, the English public did not know that "agents from the emperor of China were in Boston treating about an exchange of raw silk for wool, to be carried in Chinese junks through the Straits of Magellan."[34]

Whistling in the wind, but in every colony, especially around the five large seaports, embryo industries met the challenge that would either make or break them. Even luxury items, which fashion has always insisted must be "imported," developed sufficient *éclat* to satisfy the most particular. Advertisements such as Plunket Fleeson's of 1769, who made "AMERICAN PAPER HANGINGS, Manufactured in Philadelphia" reminded "everyone among us, who wishes prosperity to America, [to] give preference to our own manufacture, especially on the proposition, of *equally good and cheap.*"[35]

Three years later, John Hewson, with the encouragement of Benjamin Franklin, started a bleachery, dye works, and cotton printing plant, which by the time of the Revolution was so successful England placed a price of twenty guineas on Hewson's head.

In the touchy year of 1765, when young Samuel Powell was returning from his "Grand Tour" of Europe, his uncle warned him not to bring English furnishings back to Philadelphia. "Household goods may be had here as cheap & as well made from Eng. patterns. In the humor people are in here a man is in danger of becoming invidiously distinguished, who buys anything in England which our Tradesmen can furnish."[36] English patterns were well known among colonial craftsmen. In Philadelphia alone, there were at least twenty-nine copies of Thomas Chippendale's *The Gentlemen and Cabinet-maker's Director,* besides Halfpenny's *Rural Architecture in the Chinese Taste* and Sir William Chambers's *Designs of Chinese Buildings,* compiled to "stop . . . the extravagancies that daily appear under the name of Chinese, . . . most of them . . . mere inventions, the rest copies from the lame representations found on porcelain and paper hangings."[37]

Then too, there was no shortage of trained craftsmen—English, Con-

107) Philadelphia upholstered open-arm chair, its Marlboro legs carved with a Chippendale combination of Gothic and Chinese fretwork design. C. 1765.

108) Fret-galleried tea table with arched cross-stretcher. New England, 1765–75.

tinental, even an occasional local man. Also plenty of cabinet wood was available; the source of mahogany especially was closer to the colonies than to England. Yet as elegant as were the Philadelphia interpretations of Chippendale and others, there was a recognizable restraint about them often attributed to Quaker influence. Colonial furniture generally tended to be simpler than its English counterpart; however, when "Chinese Taste" was the fashion in England, it was also the fashion in the colonies. Both in Newport and Philadelphia, Chinese fretwork fenced in tea tables, ran across aprons and down square Marlboro legs. Chairbacks had pagoda crestings, the ears ending in a decided upswing.

Terminals, wherever found, were apt to repeat the roof lines of a Chinese temple.

Here and there local craftsmen translated the "Chinese Taste" into plaster frescoes around the cornice of a drawing room; built balustrades and fences of Chinese "paling"; and placed a Chinese teahouse at the end of many a garden vista, even as in England. As Benjamin Franklin

109) The Chinese fretwork staircase of "Bohemia," Eastern Shore Maryland, which follows around four sides of the entrance hall with only one panel repeated once for the sake of symmetry. C. 1745.

wrote to a friend in 1763, "After the first cares for the necessaries of life are over, we shall come to think of the embellishments . . ."[38] At the time, Franklin meant painting, poetry, and music, still he might well have said the same of the practical arts of the craftsman.

Only porcelain was the exception. Of that there was little America could learn from Europe, since Europe herself was still searching for the Chinese secret; and what was more imperative, for its ingredients. Even though there were potteries scattered from New England to Georgia, it wasn't until the early 1740s that "unaker," white clay suitable for porcelain, was discovered in the Great Smokies. By 1766, John Bartlem, one of Josiah Wedgwood's master potters who had emigrated, was sufficiently successful in South Carolina to cause Wedgwood to be "apprehensive" of losing trade to the colonies "in a few years." Before that time came, the pottery had failed. Even Bonnin and Morris, who in 1769 "introduced into this Province [Pennsylvania] a Manufacture of Porcelain or China Earthenware, . . . which by beauty and excellence, hath found its way into every refined Part of the Globe," had to close down by 1773 for lack of "generous Support."[39]

Nevertheless, enough "Friends of America" encouraged home industries to worry Great Britain, "by preferring Goods manufactured in their own Country, especially when they are as good, and sold as cheap as they can be imported from Europe."[40]

The Stamp Act was repealed in 1766; but within the year the Townshend import duties on paper, paints, lead, and tea put American men back into homespun and the women to brewing sage tea. Agitation was rife again among the merchants. Not a seacoast town but had its share of smuggling. "The Dutch, Danes, Swedes, and French," Benjamin Franklin had heard from customs officers, "now supply by smuggling the whole continent, not with tea only, but accompany that article with other India goods, . . ."[41]

Defiance phrased the Massachusetts protest of the Townshend Acts to King George III and rang through its letter to the other colonies, urging a united front. When by a vote of 92 to 17 the *"Members of the Honourable House of the* REPRESENTATIVES *of the* MASSACHUSETS-BAY" refused to recall the circular letter, the Crown summarily dissolved the body, as well as the Virginia Assembly for receiving it. Etched in silver is the memory. For on the punch bowl of his making—a gallon version of a Chinese tea bowl—Paul Revere engraved the legend *"To the Memory of the Glorious* NINETY-TWO . . . *who undaunted by the insolent Menaces of Villains in Power,* . . . VOTED NOT TO RESCIND."[42] And on a sheet of copper, Revere scratched a caricature entitled "A Warm Place—Hell," in which he pictorially castigated the seventeen miserable men who voted the King's demand.

It was Parliament who had "to rescind." The import duties were repealed, all but three pence a pound on tea. Even this token tax rankled the colonists. In the meantime the East India Company faced ruin. Franklin in London reported they had "tea and other India goods in their ware houses, to the amount of four millions, . . . for which they want a market."[43] To save its trade empire, the Company planned a tea monopoly in the colonies with government sanction, to the exclusion of local merchants. To a man, merchants rose in protest and warned England that summer of 1773, not to send over one tea ship.

Soon after, nevertheless, ships bearing half a million tons of tea sailed for Boston, New York, Philadelphia, and Charles Town. Charles Town stored the tea and allowed it to rot. New York sent it back where it came from and burned Governor Tryon's house for having said that "if orders concerning the Tea had been transmitted to him he would have landed it tho' under the mouths of the Cannon!"[44] As for Captain Ayres of the *Polly* headed for Philadelphia, he tacked back and forth off the Delaware Capes while weighing the threat of a "Halter round your Neck . . . ten Gallons of liquid Tar decanted on your Pate . . . with the Feathers of a dozen wild Geese laid over that to enliven your Appearance."[45] In the end, he sailed up the Delaware River Christmas Day into the middle of the news about Boston's "Tea Party."

They said there were about two hundred that marched two by two to Griffin's wharf on the sixteenth of December, in Boston, to where three ships each had "114 chests of the *ill-fated* article on board." They said they were *"Indians* from *Narragansett.* Whether they were or not, . . . [they were] cloathed in blankets with the heads muffled, and copper-colored countenances, . . . each armed with a hatchet or axe, and pair pistols, . . . their jargon . . . unintelligible to all but themselves . . ." "Before *nine* o'clock in the evening, every chest from on board the three vessels was knocked to pieces and flung over the sides."[46]

Captain Ayres was lucky that he could sail his brig away again from

110) German version of the Boston Tea Party, December 16, 1773. Engraved by D. Berger, 1784, after D. Chodowiecki.

Philadelphia, that neither this catchy jingle nor its implications were turned on him:

> *Rally, Mohawks! bring out your axes,*
> *And tell King George we'll pay no taxes*
> *On his foreign tea;*
> *His threats are vain, and vain to think*
> *To force our girls and wives to drink*
> *His vile Bohea!*[47]

But for Boston, the tea fracas brought down the wrath of Parliament. On the 31st of March 1774, George III signed the Boston Port Bill, which gave the colonists until June first to come to their senses, else the port would be closed to all traffic. With indignation, one colony after another came to the support of the beleaguered town. New Hampshire promptly organized volunteers. Maryland, then New Jersey, supported the suspension of trade with England. And from South Carolina and Virginia rolled up a thunderous volume of defiance. From one end of the Atlantic seaboard to the other, however, the immediate natural reaction of individuals was against the precipitator of the crisis, tea.

With the inevitable closing of Boston harbor on the first of June, tea became a symbol, the "forbidden herb." Barely a month thereafter, John Adams, on his way to the First Continental Congress, asked at an inn in Falmouth, "Is it lawful for a weary traveller to refresh himself with a dish of tea, provided it has been honestly smuggled, or paid no duties?" "No, sir," came the quick answer, "we have renounced all tea in this place, but I'll make you coffee."[48] So it was in Philadelphia, where Peggy Shippen "searched every Shop in town for a blue & white China Coffee Pot, but no such thing is to be had, nor indeed any other sort that can be called handsome; since the disuse of Tea great Numbers of people have been endeavouring to supply themselves with Coffee Pots . . . without success."[49]

In Virginia, too, everyone drank coffee, as Philip Fithian, tutor to the children of Robert Carter of Nomini Hall wrote in his diary, "they are now too patriotic to use tea, . . ."[50] In fact, even "before the Day came"—the first of June—the ladies made quite a ceremony of sealing up the tea "which they had on hand and vowed never to use it till the oppressive Act imposing a Duty thereon should be repealed."[51] Up and down the colonies, newspapers printed "A lady's Adieu to her Tea-Table," which ran in part:

> *Farewell the Teaboard with your gaudy attire,*
> *Ye cups and saucers that I did admire;*
> *To my cream pot and tongs I now bid adieu;*
> *That pleasure's all fled that I once found in you . . .*
> *No more shall my teapot so generous be*
> *In filling the cups with this pernicious tea,*
> *For I'll fill it with water and drink out the same,*
> *Before I'll lose LIBERTY that dearest name . . .*[52]

On Christmas morning, 1775, Fithian wrote: "*Tea* is out of the Question; it is almost Treason against the Country to mention it, much more to drink it."[53]

The last "tea fleet" had sailed out of England. With it had gone

III) English caricature of the Ladies of Edenton, North Carolina, who "do hereby Solemnly Engage not to Conform to that Pernicious Custom of Drinking Tea, or that we the afore-said Ladys will not promote yᵉ wear of any Manufacture from England untill such time that all Acts which tend to Enslave this our Native Country shall be Repealed." A mezzotint by Philip Dawe, 1775.

forever the strength of the Company, that East India Company which was fed on the "advantages and benefitts to trade" Catherine of Braganza had brought to England in her dowry. With the end of the American Revolution, it was the newborn United States that now adventured into the China trade. Even as Michel de Crèvecœur had written, "Americans are the western pilgrims, who are carrying along with them that great mass of arts, sciences, vigour, and industry which began long since in the east; they will finish the great circle."[54]

Less than three months after the British had evacuated New York on November 25, 1783, the American *Empress of China* sailed out of that harbor for Canton, in the wake of two centuries of East India ships. The years had but slightly polished relations between East and West. Much the same system of trade applied to "second chop Englishmen" as had irritated previous generations of "red-haired devils." Nevertheless, fourteen months later, in the spring of 1785, the wharves of New York were piled as deep as any in London with the rich, aromatic trade goods out of the holds of the *Empress of China*.

Besides chests of symbolic tea—Bohea, Hyson, and Gunpowder*— there were tubs and boxes of chinaware, tea and "table" china, "cyphered," and "blue and white"; lacquer-ware; sets of mother-of-pearl "fish" counters and ciphered ones; "ombrellas" large and small; malacca canes and whangees; musk and fans; and cases of "Sundry sorts of Silk," striped, flowered, and "Silver sprig'd Embroidered White Lutestring," silks in colors that ran the gamut of ash, straw, celadon, pea and olive green, light and dark blue, cherry, crimson, claret, puce, and changeable.[55]

The trade of the world, as well as the arts and mysteries of the East, lay now at the feet of an infant nation. Even as in England before, direct contact revived again the vogue for things from the East. A bit diluted and tawdry from two hundred years of commercial contact with the West, they nevertheless exuded again their exotic charms on a new land. As American "China Ships" and "Clippers" sailed the ancient lanes of trade, the whole world watched a vast new era begin.

---

* *Small or broken tea leaves rolled into tiny pellets hardly as large as a peppercorn.*

Notes

CHAPTER ONE

1. Samuel Pepys: *Diary and Correspondence of Samuel Pepys* (London: Hurst and Blackett; 1854), May 16, 1660.
2. Thomas Carte: *An History of the life of James, duke of Ormonde,* 2 vols. (London, 1736). As quoted in Lillias C. Davidson, *Catherine of Bragança* (London: John Murray; 1908), p. 48.
3. Earl of Clarendon: *Life of Edward, Earl of Clarendon, Written by Himself* (Oxford: Clarendon Printing House; 1759), Vol. II, p. 168.
4. T. H. Lister: *Life and Administration of Edward, First Earl of Clarendon* (London: Longman, Orme, Brown, Green, and Longman; 1837), Vol. III, p. 156.
5. Ibid.
6. H. S. a Cosmopolite: *Iter Lusitanicum: or The Portugal Voyage* (London, 1662), pp. 24, 25.
7. Manuel Komroff, ed.: *The Travels of Marco Polo* (New York: Garden City Publishing Co.; 1930), p. 272.
8. "Prester John," *Encyclopaedia Britannica,* 14th edition, Vol. XVIII, p. 459.
9. "Age of Exploration," *Life,* Vol. XXIV, No. 12 (March 22, 1948), as quoted on p. 97.
10. Henry S. Lucas: *The Renaissance and the Reformation* (New York: Harper & Bros.; 1934), as quoted on p. 350.
11. "Japan," *Encyclopaedia Britannica,* Vol. XII, as quoted on p. 939.
12. Clarendon's *Life,* Vol. II. p. 152.
13. Ibid. p. 149.
14. Pepys's *Diary,* May 24, 1662.
15. Clarendon's *Life,* Vol. II, p. 316.

16. Pepys's *Diary*, June 3, 1662.

17. Ibid. June 5, 1662.

18. Lister: *Life and Administration of Edward, First Earl of Clarendon,* Vol. III, p. 197. Quoted from original MS. in the British Museum, Lansdowne MSS., 1236.

19. Ibid.

CHAPTER TWO

1. Richard Hakluyt: *The Principal Navigations, Voyages, Traffiques & Discoveries of the English Nation* (1600) (New York: MacLehose, of Glasgow, and Macmillan; 1904), p. 113.

2. Ibid. pp. 116, 117.

3. Ibid. p. 116

4. As quoted in Ethel B. Sainsbury: *A Calendar of The Court Minutes, etc., of the East India Company, 1640–1643* (Oxford: Clarendon Press; 1907–1938) A Court of Sales and a General Court, October 30, 1640. (Court Book, Vol. XVII, p. 327), pp. 106, 107.

5. Ibid. p. 114.

6. Ibid. A Court of Committees, Nov. 25, 1640 (Court Book, Vol. XVII, p. 348), p. 114.

7. Ibid. A Court of Committees, June 3, 1640 (Court Book, Vol. XVII, p. 190), as quoted on p. 45.

8. Ibid. February 21, 1640, as quoted on p. 18.

9. *The Diary of John Evelyn* (New York: Everyman's Library; 1950), February 19, 1652.

10. As quoted in *The Pennsylvania Chronicle*, No. 59, February 22–9, 1768.

11. Lucy Hutchinson: *Memoirs of Colonel Hutchinson.* As quoted in Millia Davenport: *The Book of Costume* (New York: Crown; 1948), p. 576.

12. Sainsbury, *Calendar of Court Minutes, 1674–1676*, p. 356.

CHAPTER THREE

1. Lister: *Life and Administration of Edward, First Earl of Clarendon,* Vol. III, p. 197. Original MS. in the British Museum, Lansdowne MSS., 1236.

2. Evelyn's *Diary*, May 30, 1662.

3. Ibid. August 23, 1662.

4. Pepys's *Diary*, November 16, 1665.

5. Evelyn's *Diary,* April 17, 1673.

6. Ibid. December 18, 1682.

7. Sainsbury, *Calendar of Court Minutes, 1660–1663,* pp. 102, 103.

8. Excerpt of "Order of Council, March 6, 1668" (Public Record Office: Privy Council Register, Vol. IX, p. 216). As quoted in Sainsbury, *Calendar of Court Minutes, 1668–1670,* p. 35.

9. As quoted in Hosea Ballow Morse: *The Chronicle of the East India Company Trading to China: 1635–1834* (Cambridge: Harvard University Press; 1926), Vol. I, p. 29.

10. Ibid. p. 98.

11. As quoted in "Japan," *Encyclopaedia Britannica,* Vol. XII, p. 940.

12. Anthony Hamilton: *Memoirs of Count Gramont* (London: Chatto & Windus; 1876), p. 102.

13. Pepys's *Diary,* September 7, 1662.

14. Gilbert Burnet: *Bishop Burnet's History of His Own Time: from the Restoration of Charles II to the Treaty of Peace at Utrecht, in the Reign of Queen Anne* (London: William Smith; 1847), Vol. I, p. 236.

15. Pepys's *Diary,* October 24, 1662.

16. Hamilton, *Memoirs of Count Grammont,* p. 126.

17. Pepys's *Diary,* June 23, 1663.

CHAPTER FOUR

1. Daniel Defoe: *The Review* of 1708. As quoted in M. D. C. Crawford: *The Heritage of Cotton* (New York: Grosset & Dunlap; 1924), p. 98.

2. Clarendon's *Life,* Vol. II, p. 319.

3. Hamilton, *Memoirs of Count Gramont,* p. 102.

4. Pepys's *Diary,* July 12, 1663.

5. Horace Walpole: *Anecdotes of Painting in England* (London: Chatto & Windus; 1876), Vol. II, p. 91.

6. Pepys's *Diary,* October 20, 1666.

7. Excerpt from pamphlet, "The Weavers' True Case," 1719. As quoted in Crawford, *Heritage of Cotton,* p. 101.

8. Excerpt of letter from Sir Thomas Roe, English ambassador to Mughal Court, 1615–1619, dated April 25, 1617. *Letters Received by the East India Company, 1617,* W. Foster, ed. (London, 1902), p. 200. As quoted in John Irwin: "Indian Textile Trade in the 17th Century, I—Western India," *Journal of Indian Textile History* (Ahmedabad, India), Vol. I (1955), p. 7.

9. Excerpt of letter from the Company to Surat, November 1643. As quoted in Sainsbury, "Introduction," *Calendar of Court Minutes, 1644–1649,* p. iii.

10. *India Office Archives, Letter Book III,* p. 161. As quoted in John Irwin: "The Origins of the 'Oriental Style' in English Decorative Art," *Burlington Magazine,* Vol. XCVII (April 1955), p. 109.

11. Evelyn's *Diary,* December 30, 1665.

12. *Records of Fort St. George: Despatches from England, 1681–1686* (Madras, 1916), p. 31. As quoted in John Irwin: "Indian Textile Trade in the 17th Century, II—Coromandel Coast," *Journal of Indian Textile History,* Vol. II (1956), p. 31.

13. This paragraph is based on Père Cœurdoux's report in *Lettres Edifiantes et Curieuses,* Vol. XIV. As quoted in G. P. Baker: *Calico Painting and Printing in the East Indies in the XVIIth and XVIIIth Centuries* (London: Edward Arnold; 1921), pp. 11, 12.

14. Genesis 3:22, 23.

15. This paragraph is based on Père Cœurdoux's letters, as quoted in Baker, *Calico Painting and Printing in the East Indies,* p. 13.

16. Ibid. p. 14.

17. Ibid. pp. 15, 16.

18. Dr. Havart: *Rise and Fall of Coromandel* (Amsterdam, 1693). As quoted in Baker, *Calico Painting and Printing in the East Indies,* p. 21.

19. Excerpt of letter from Lords Commissioners of His Majesty's Ordnance to the Company. As quoted in Sainsbury: *Calendar of Court Minutes, 1668–1670,* September 17, 1669 (Court Book, Vol. XXVI, p. 526), p. 241.

20. This paragraph is based on Sainsbury: *Calendar of Court Minutes, 1640–1643* (Court Book, Vol. XVII, p. 327), p. 105; and *1668–1670* (Court Book, Vol. XXVI, p. 474), p. 209.

21. Pepys's *Diary,* December 12, 1663.

22. Ibid. November 21, 1663.

23. *India Office Archives, Letter Book VII,* p. 136. As quoted in Irwin: "Indian Textile Trade in the 17th Century, II," *Journal of Indian Textile History,* Vol. II, p. 31.

24. Excerpt of Company letter to Surat factors, 1683, *India Office Archives, Letter Book VII,* p. 210. As quoted, ibid. Vol. I, p. 15.

25. Excerpt of letter of 1686, *India Office Archives, Letter Book VIII,* p. 275. As quoted in Crawford, *Heritage of Cotton,* p. 96.

26. Pepys's *Diary,* March 30, 1666.

27. Edward Chamberlayne: *Angliae Notitia or The Present State of England,* 15th edition (London, 1684), pp. 179, 226.

28. Daniel Defoe: *The Review* of 1708. As quoted in Crawford, *Heritage of Cotton,* p. 98.

29. Ibid.

30. Alexander Pope: *Moral Essays,* Epistle 1. As quoted in John Ashton: *Social Life in the Reign of Queen Anne* (London: Chatto & Windus; 1893), p. 37.

31. Excerpt from a political speech by "Pollexfen" in 1681 before the Board of Trade. *India Office Library Tracts,* Vol. LXXXIII, p. 50. As quoted in Irwin: "Indian Textile Trade in the 17th Century, I," *Journal of Indian Textile History,* Vol. I, p. 10.

32. Excerpt from a pamphlet, "The Naked Truth, in an Essay upon Trade," 1696. As quoted in Crawford, *Heritage of Cotton,* p. 98.

33. Transcript of unidentified newspaper clipping in the possession of Harvard College Library, *Theatre Collection,* Cambridge, Mass., which also owns a manuscript draft letter of the same, dated "Adelphi June 2," of the year 1775.

34. Excerpt from the answer of the Secretary of the Customs, Sir Guy Cooper. As quoted in Baker, *Calico Painting and Printing in the East Indies,* pp. 7, 8.

35. John Taylor (the "Water Poet"): "The Needles Excellency," 1640. As quoted in A. F. Kendrick: *English Needlework* (London: A. & C. Black; 1933), p. 117.

36. Lady Llanover, ed.: *The Autobiography and Correspondence of Mary Granville, Mrs. Delany* (London: Richard Bentley; 1861), 1st series, Vol. II, p. 147.

37. Excerpt from a political pamphlet dated 1782. As quoted in G. M. Trevelyan: *Illustrated English Social History* (London: Longmans, Green; 1951), Vol. III, p. 94.

38. *The Gentleman's Magazine,* October 3, 1763, p. 514.

39. *Boston Gazette,* June 16–23, 1735. As quoted in George Francis Dow: *The Arts and Crafts in New England, 1704–1775* (Topsfield, Mass.: The Wayside Press; 1927), p. 258.

40. *Harvard College Records,* 2, p. 62.

CHAPTER FIVE

1. From paragraph 2 of the Cane-Makers' reply to the Wool-Workers' petition to Parliament to prohibit the making of cane chairs. As quoted by R. W. Symonds: "English Cane Chairs," Part I, *The Connoisseur,* CXXVII, p. 520 (April 1951), p. 13.

2. Clarendon's *Life,* Vol. II, p. 330.

3. Evelyn's *Diary,* February 4, 1685.

4. Ibid.

5. Pepys's *Diary,* February 14, 1668.

6. Ibid. October 21, 1663.

7. Ibid. October 20, 1663.

8. Ibid. November 2, 1663.

9. As quoted in Pepys's *Diary,* October 20, 1663, note.

10. "Price Butler's Tale, 1669." As quoted in Esther Singleton: *Dutch and Flemish Furniture* (New York: McClure; 1902), pp. 290, 291.

11. From invoice as quoted in Symonds: "English Cane Chairs," Part II, *The Connoisseur,* CXXVII, p. 521 (June 1951), p. 83.

12. Evelyn's *Diary,* February 4, 1685.

13. Pepys's *Diary,* September 2, 1667.

14. Ibid. August 24, 1667.

15. Playing card in Worcester College, Oxford University.

16. Samuel Sewall: *Letter Book, 1686–1729.* Collections of the Massachusetts Historical Society, 6th series (Boston, 1888), Vol. II, p. 106.

17. A. C. Prime: *The Arts and Crafts in Philadelphia* (Topsfield, Mass.: Walpole Society; 1929), Vol. I, p. 167. His name was Nicholas Gale.

CHAPTER SIX

1. P. J. B. du Halde: *A Description of the Empire of China,* trans. from the French (London, 1738), Vol. I, p. 9.

2. John Nieuhoff: *An Embassy from the East India Company of the United Provinces to the Grand Tartar Cham Emperor of China* (London, 1673).

3. Evelyn's *Diary,* December 4, 1679.

4. Louis Le Compte: *Memoirs and Observations* (London, 1697), p. 152.

5. Ibid. p. 152.

6. John Stalker: *A Treatise of Japanning and Varnishing, Being a Compleat Discovery of Those Arts* (Oxford, 1688), p. 38.

7. Evelyn's *Diary,* July 30, 1682.

8. Du Halde, *Description of the Empire of China,* pp. i, ii.

9. *East India Company Letter Book of 1697,* p. 169. As quoted in Margaret Jourdain & R. Soame Jenyns: *Chinese Export Art in the 18th Century* (London: Country Life; 1950), p. 69.

10. Pepys's *Diary,* May 23, 1663.

11. *Memoirs of the Verney Family* (London, 1892–99), Vol. IV, p. 221. As quoted in B. Sprague Allen: *Tides in English Taste* (1619–1800), (Cambridge: Harvard University Press; 1937), Vol. I, p. 203.

12. As quoted in Singleton, *Dutch and Flemish Furniture*, p. 289.

13. Stalker, *Treatise*, p. 36.

14. The Earl of Rochester: *Poems* (London, 1702).

15. Stalker, *Treatise*, "Epistle."

16. September 9, 1729, *The Autobiography and Correspondence of Mary Granville, Mrs. Delany*, 1st series, Vol. I, p. 213.

17. Dow, *Arts and Crafts in New England*, p. 237.

18. *Diary of Samuel Sewall*, 1673–1729. Collections of the Massachusetts Historical Society, 5th series (Boston, 1878), January 29, 1711–12, p. 333.

19. As quoted in Joseph Downs: *American Furniture* (New York: Macmillan; 1952), p. 188.

20. Dow, *Arts and Crafts in New England*, p. 297.

21. Rita Susswein Gottesman: *The Arts and Crafts in New York, 1726–1776* (New York: New-York Historical Society; 1938), p. 120.

22. Du Halde, *Description of the Empire of China*, p. 277.

CHAPTER SEVEN

1. Pepys's *Diary*, January 1, 1663/4.

2. Excerpt of a letter from Charles II to his sister, the Duchess of Orleans, February 9, 1663. As quoted in Julia Cartwright: *Madame* (New York: Dutton; 1901), p. 132.

3. Pepys's *Diary*, November 15, 1666.

4. Excerpt of a letter dated "Whitehall, 9/Feb./'63." Cartwright, *Madame*, p. 132.

5. Excerpt of letter quoted in Hamilton, *Memoirs of Count Gramont*, p. 284, note.

6. Excerpt of letter of Lady Chaworth dated September 7, 1675. "Duke of Rutland," *Historical Manuscripts Commission*, Vol. II, p. 27. As quoted in Arthur Bryant: *King Charles II* (London: Longmans, Green; 1934), p. 244.

7. Excerpt of letter from Lord Cornbury to the Marchioness of Worcester, June 10, 1662. Eliot Warburton: *Memoirs of Prince Rupert*, Vol. III, p. 461. As quoted in Pepys's *Diary*, February 8, 1663, note.

8. "Mercurious Politicus" No. 435, September 1658. As quoted in "Tea," *Encyclopaedia Britannica*, Vol. XXI, p. 857.

9. As quoted in Gervas Huxley: *Talking of Tea* (London: Thames & Hudson; 1956), pp. 67, 68.

10. Albert Jacquemart: *History of the Ceramic Art* (New York: Scribner, Armstrong; 1877), p. 44.

11. Pepys's *Diary*, September 25, 1660.

12. Ibid. June 28, 1667.

13. Edmund Waller: *Poems, &c.* (London, 1712), p. 228.

14. Pepys's *Diary*, August 14, 1666.

15. Ibid. October 13, 1660.

16. Ibid. May 28, 1667.

17. Mr. Hxxxx: "An Essay on Tea," 1757. As quoted in Christian Hole: *English Home-Life: 1500–1800* (London: B. T. Batsford; 1949), p. 110.

18. As quoted in Huxley, *Talking of Tea*, p. 70.

19. *Literary Magazine*, Vol. II, No. XII, 1757. As quoted in *Oxford Dictionary of Quotations*, p. 278.

20. As quoted in Huxley, *Talking of Tea*, p. 70.

21. This paragraph is based on W. S. Scott: *Bygone Pleasures of London* (London: Marsland Publications; 1948). The quotations are to be found on pp. 14, 16, 19.

22. Pepys's *Diary*, May 28, 1667.

23. *The Spectator*, No. 383, May 20, 1712.

24. *London and its Environs Described* (London: Printed for R. & J. Dodsley in Pall-Mall; 1761), Vol. VI, pp. 214, 215. As quoted in John Gloag: *Georgian Grace* (New York: Macmillan; 1956), p. 172.

25. Horace Walpole to George Montagu, June 23, 1750. *The Letters of Horace Walpole, Earl of Orford*, Peter Cunningham, ed., 9 vols. (London: Bentley; 1859).

26. Ibid. Horace Walpole to Horace Mann, May 26, 1742.

27. *The Tatler*, No. 148, Tuesday, March 21, 1710.

28. Thomas Bount: *Glossographia*, 2nd edition (1661). As quoted in Charles Oman: *English Domestic Silver* (London: Adam & Charles Black; 1949), p. 132.

29. *The Tatler*, No. 166, May 2, 1710.

30. *The Works of Thomas Brown* (1719 edition), Vol. III, p. 86. As quoted in John Ashton, *Social Life in the Reign of Queen Anne*, p. 73.

31. As quoted in Agnes Repplier: *To Think of Tea!* (Boston: Houghton Mifflin; 1932), p. 67.

32. Arthur Young's "Farmer's Letters" (1767). As quoted in Trevelyan, *Illustrated English Social History*, Vol. III, p. 91.

33. John Cookley Lettson: *The Natural History of the Tea-Tree* (London, 1772), p. 63.

34. The Rev. James Woodforde: *The Diary of a Country Parson*, J. D. Beresford, ed. As quoted in Hole, *English Home-Life*, p. 113.

35. As quoted in Repplier, *To Think of Tea!* p. 43.

36. Horace Walpole: *Memoirs of the Reign of King George the Third* (New York: G. P. Putnam's Sons; 1894), Vol. III, p. 136.

37. Lord Chancellor Hyde to the Earl of St. Albans, April 8, 1661. Quoted from original MS. in Bodeleian Library, Oxford. Lister, *Life and Administration of Edward, First Earl of Clarendon*, Vol. III, pp. 119–24.

38. Benjamin Franklin to Thomas Cushing, London, 5 January 1773. As quoted in Benjamin Franklin: *The Life and Letters of Benjamin Franklin* (Eau Claire, Wisc.: E. M. Hale; n.d.), p. 196.

39. Walpole, *Memoirs of the Reign of King George the Third*, Vol. III, p. 16.

40. As quoted in Huxley, *Talking of Tea*, p. 95.

CHAPTER EIGHT

1. Excerpt from Pierre de la Noue's 1617 translation of the original Latin. As quoted in Jacquemart, *History of the Ceramic Art*, p. 75.

2. Marco Polo: *The Travels of Marco Polo*, pp. 225, 226.

3. As quoted in Jacquemart, *History of the Ceramic Art*, p. 75.

4. Ibid.

5. Celia Fiennes: *Through England on a Side Saddle in the Time of William and Mary* (London: Field; 1888). As quoted in Huxley, *Talking of Tea*, p. 92.

6. Blencowe: *Diary of the Times of Charles II*. As quoted in Cartwright, *Madame*, p. 299.

7. Evelyn's *Diary*, September 6, 1662.

8. Daniel Defoe: *A Tour Through England and Wales* (New York: E. P. Dutton; 1928), Vol. I, Letter III, p. 175.

9. Ibid.

10. Ibid. Vol. I, Letter II, p. 166.

11. Ibid.

12. As quoted in J. A. Lloyd Hyde and Ricardo R. Espirito: *Chinese Porcelain for the European Market* (Lisbon: R. E. S. M.; 1956), p. 52.

13. This paragraph is based on the actual inventory of the *Macclesfield* out of Canton, 1700. Morse, *Chronicles of the East India Company*, p. 97.

14. The Lord Chancellor Hyde to the Earl of St. Albans, April 8, 1661. As quoted in Lister, *Life and Administration of Edward, First Earl of Clarendon*, Vol. III, pp. 119–24.

15. *The Lover*, No. 10, March 18, 1714, *Works of Joseph Addison* (New York: Harper; 1837), Vol. III.

16. Francis Bacon: "The Case of Impeachment of Waste," *The Works of Francis Bacon,* Vol. V of *Literary and Professional Works* (Boston: Houghton Mifflin), p. 37.

17. This paragraph is based on the letters of Père d' Entrecolles, as quoted in du Halde, *Description of the Empire of China,* Vol. I, pp. 339–42.

18. *The Lover,* No. 10, Thursday, March 18, 1714.

19. Harleian MSS. 5996, 147. As quoted in Ashton, *Social Life in the Reign of Queen Anne,* p. 57.

20. Du Halde, *Description of the Empire of China,* Vol. I, p. 343.

21. Le Compte, *Memoirs,* p. 157.

22. Ibid. p. 126.

23. Charles Lamb: "Old China," *The Essays of Elia* (London: Macmillan; 1903).

24. From the patent application of John Dwight. As quoted in Eliza Meteyard: *Life and Works of Wedgwood* (London: Hurst and Blackett; 1865), Vol. I, p. 108.

25. From a letter of William Cookworthy of Plymouth to a friend in 1745. As quoted in George Savage: *Porcelain Through the Ages* (Harmondsworth, Eng.: Pelican Books; 1954), p. 216.

26. From the patent for porcelain making petitioned by Edward Heylyn and Thomas Frye in 1744. As quoted, ibid. p. 216.

27. Daniel Defoe: *The Review,* No. 43. As quoted in Allen, *Tides in English Taste,* p. 191.

28. *The Spectator,* No. 552.

29. Ibid. No. 288.

30. Excerpt of a letter from Franklin to his wife, dated London, February 19, 1758. As quoted in *The Life and Letters of Benjamin Franklin,* p. 191.

31. Ibid. pp. 118, 117.

32. Franklin's "Autobiography," ibid. p. 52.

33. Ibid.

34. As quoted in John Spargo: *Early American Pottery and China* (New York: Century; 1926), p. 64.

35. From the 1688 description of the pottery works and "one million of Acres" belonging to "Daniel Coxe proprietary and Governor of ye provinces of East and West Jersey in America," as quoted, ibid. p. 56. Original in Rawlinson Collection, Bodleian Library, Oxford.

36. As quoted, ibid., p. 65.

37. As quoted, ibid., p. 76.

38. From a letter "To an engraver," London, November 3, 1773. As quoted in *The Life and Letters of Benjamin Franklin,* p. 204.

39. *New York Weekly Chronicle*, March 5, 1795. As quoted in Gottesman, *Arts and Crafts in New York*, Vol. II, p. 13.

40. From "Hints for Tea Parties, etc.," *Scribner's Monthly and Illustrated Magazine for the People*, 1875, gathered from unnamed letters and journals dating between 1794 and 1797. As quoted in *Food, Entertainment and Decorations of the Table*, p. 16. Colonial Williamsburg Research Library.

CHAPTER NINE

1. James Cawthorne: "Essays on Taste" (1756), *Poems* (London, 1771). As quoted in William W. Appleton: *A Cycle of Cathay* (New York: Columbia University Press; 1951), p. 90.

2. As quoted in Sainsbury, *Calendar of Court Minutes, 1674–1676*, p. xix.

3. Clarendon's *Life*, Vol. II, p. 149.

4. Excerpt from "An Answer to two letters concerning the East India Company, Bristol, June 30, 1676" [British Museum, 1029.g.22(2)]. As quoted in Sainsbury, *Calendar of Court Minutes, 1674–1676*, p. 325.

5. Waller, *Poems, &c.*, p. 227.

6. Pepys's *Diary*, May 28, 1665.

7. Ibid. June 25, 1666.

8. Evelyn's *Diary*, September 25, 1679.

9. Excerpt from letter dated September, 1689. Egerton, I. 534, Letter 36. As quoted in Davidson, *Catherine of Bragança*, p. 437.

10. Excerpt from letter of Lady Gardiner to Sir John Verney, September 5, 1699. As quoted in Margaret Maria Lady Verney, ed.: *Verney Letters of the 18th Century, from the MSS at Claydon House* (London, 1930), 2 vols., Vol. I, p. 44.

11. Stalker, *Treatise of Japanning and Varnishing*, Preface.

12. Pepys's *Diary*, February 12, 1667.

13. Quoted in E. K. Chambers: *The Elizabethan Stage* (Oxford: Clarendon Press; 1923), Vol. III, p. 279.

14. This paragraph is based on Appleton, *A Cycle of Cathay*, pp. 70, 71, from which is also the quotation from *The Fairy Queen*, V, ii.

15. T. Baker: *The Fine Lady's Airs* (1708). As quoted in E. F. Carritt, ed.: *A Calendar of British Taste* (London: Routledge & Kegan Paul; 1948), p. 149.

16. William Hickey, *Memoirs*. As quoted in Margaret Jourdain & R. Soame Jenyns, *Chinese Export Art* (London: Country Life Ltd; 1950), p. 12.

17. Peter Osbeck: *A Voyage to China and the East Indies* (London, 1771), Vol. I, p. 119, 120.

18. Ibid.

19. Sir George Staunton, as quoted in John Goldsmith Phillips: *China-Trade Porcelain* (Cambridge: Harvard University Press; 1956), p. 14.

20. Du Halde, *Description of the Empire of China,* Vol. II, p. 280.

21. Le Compte, *A Description of China.* As quoted in Smart, Goldsmith, & Johnson, eds.: *The World Displayed; or a Curious Collection of Voyages and Travels,* 1st American edition (Philadelphia, 1795), Vol. VI, p. 237.

22. Evelyn's *Diary,* July 23, 1700.

23. Defoe, *Tour Through England and Wales,* Vol. I, pp. 6 and 15.

24. William Hogarth: *Analysis of Beauty.* As quoted in Caritt, *A Calendar of British Taste,* p. 263.

25. Horace Walpole to Horace Mann, February 25, 1750. As quoted, ibid. p. 251.

26. Sir William Temple, "Essay on Gardening," 1685. As quoted in John Gloag: *Georgian Grace* (New York: Macmillan; 1956), p. 110.

27. Sir William Chambers: *Designs of Chinese Buildings, Furniture, Dresses, Machines, and Utensils* (London, 1757), p. 15.

28. Temple, "Essay on Gardening."

29. Peter Osbeck, as quoted in Lettsom, *The Natural History of the Tea-Tree,* p. 9.

30. Excerpt from a letter to Mrs. Dewes, April 22, 1752. *Autobiography of Mary Granville, Mrs. Delany,* 1st series (New York: Dover Publications; 1948), Vol. III, p. 112.

31. Parts of this paragraph based on George N. Kates: *Chinese Household Furniture* (New York: Harper and Brothers; 1948).

32. Excerpt from letter to Mrs. Dewes, October 30, 1746. *Autobiography of Mary Granville, Mrs. Delany,* 1st series, Vol. II, p. 441.

33. Emily Climenson, ed.: *Passages from the Diaries of Mrs. Philip Lybbe Powys, A.D. 1756–1808* (London: Longmans, Green; 1899), p. 63. This was "Eastbury," near Salisbury, 1760.

34. Chambers, *Designs of Chinese Buildings,* p. 10.

35. Thomas Chippendale: *The Gentleman and Cabinet Maker's Director: Being a large Collection of the Most Elegant and Useful Designs of Household Furniture, in the Most Fashionable Taste,* 3rd edition (London, 1762), Plates XXVI, XXVII, XXVIII.

36. Ibid.

37. John Baptist Jackson: *An Essay on the Invention of Engraving and*

Printing in Chiaro Oscuro. As quoted in Jourdain and Jenyns, *Chinese Export Art,* p. 26.

38. Excerpt of a letter to "Sarah," dated January 3, 1750. Emily J. Climenson: *Elizabeth Montagu, The Queen of the Blue Stockings, 1720–1761* (London: John Murray; 1906), Vol. I, p. 271.

39. John Shebbeare: *Letters on the English Nation* (London, 1755) Vol. II, Letter LVI, "The taste of England at present in architecture."

40. Le Compte, *A Description of China.* As quoted in Smart, Goldsmith & Johnson, *The World Displayed,* Vol. VI, p. 184.

41. Le Compte, *Memoirs,* p. 128.

42. *The World,* No. XII (London, 1753).

43. Shebbeare, *Letters on the English Nation,* Vol. II, Letter LVI.

44. Robert Morris: *The Architectural Remembrancer* (London; 1751). As quoted in Carritt, *Calendar of British Taste,* p. 257.

45. Peter Osbeck: *A Voyage to China and the East Indies,* trans. from the German by John R. Forster (London, 1771), 2 vols., Vol. I, p. 231.

46. Climenson, *Elizabeth Montagu,* Vol, I, p. 271.

47. This paragraph is based on Jane Campbell: *The Story of the Willow Plate* (Philadelphia, n.d.).

48. *The World,* No. XII.

49. Arthur Young, as quoted in J. H. Plumb: *England in the Eighteenth Century* (Harmondsworth, Eng.: Pelican Books; 1950), p. 143.

50. Defoe, as quoted, ibid. p. 21.

51. Clarendon's *Life,* Vol. II, p. 149.

52. The Earl of Sandwich, as quoted in *The American Heritage Book of the Revolution* (New York: American Heritage; 1958), p. 27.

53. Peter Cunningham, ed.: *The Letters of Horace Walpole, Earl of Orford* (London: Richard Bentley; 1858), Vol. VII, p. 275.

CHAPTER TEN

1. As quoted in Edward P. Cheyney: *A Short History of England* (Boston: Ginn; 1945), p. 286.

2. As quoted in Esther Singleton: *Dutch New York* (New York: Dodd, Mead; 1909), p. 137.

3. Ibid. p. 85.

4. Dr. Alexander Hamilton: *Gentleman's Progress,* Carl Bridenbaugh, ed. (Chapel Hill: University of North Carolina Press; 1948), p. 72.

5. As quoted in Singleton, *Dutch New York,* p. 335.

6. Ibid. p. 339.

7. Ibid. p. 337.

8. Ibid. p. 338.

9. John Higginson: *The Cause of God and His People in New England* (1663), Colonial Society of Massachusetts, *Publications,* Vol. I, p. 398. As quoted in Thomas Jefferson Wertenbaker: *The First Americans* (New York: Macmillan; 1929), p. 112.

10. From Samuel Torrey's election sermon, 1674, Weymouth, Mass., in Lindsay Swift: *The Massachusetts Election Sermons,* Colonial Society of Massachusetts, *Publications,* Vol. I, p. 402. As quoted in Wertenbaker, *The First Americans,* p. 110.

11. As quoted in Hiram Bingham: *Elihu Yale* (New York: Dodd, Mead; 1939), p. 324.

12. Ibid.

13. Daniel Neal: *The History of New England* (London, 1720), Vol. II, p. 590.

14. Ibid. p. 614.

15. Samuel Sewall's *Letter Book,* Collections of the Massachusetts Historical Society, 6th series, Vol. II, p. 106.

16. As quoted in Esther Singleton: *The Furniture of our Forefathers* (New York: Doubleday, Page; 1900), Vol. II, p. 374.

17. Hugh Jones: *The Present State of Virginia* (Chapel Hill: University of North Carolina Press; 1956), p. 73.

18. Robert Beverley: *The History and Present State of Virginia* (Chapel Hill: University of North Carolina Press; 1947), p. 295.

19. Jones, *The Present State of Virginia,* p. 71.

20. As quoted in Jared Sparks: *The Writings of George Washington* (Boston: Ferdinand Andrews; 1839), Vol. II, p. 329n.

21. Jones, *The Present State of Virginia,* p. 71.

22. William Byrd: "Progress to the Mines" (1732), from *The London Diary* (1717–1721), Louis B. Wright and Marion Tinling, ed. (New York: Oxford University Press; 1958), p. 628.

23. As quoted in Marshall B. Davidson: *Life in America* (Boston: Houghton Mifflin; 1951), Vol. I, p. 66.

24. Governor Glen, as quoted in Carl Bridenbaugh: *Cities in Revolt* (New York: Knopf; 1955), p. 143.

25. Pepys's *Diary,* August 30, 1664.

26. George Fox: "An Additional Extract from Other of George Fox's Epistles," *Works,* Vol. VII, p. 345. As quoted in Frederick B. Tolles: *Meeting House and Counting House* (Chapel Hill: University of North Carolina Press; 1948), p. 55.

27. Thomas Pownall, as quoted in Harold D. Eberlein and Cortlandt V. Hubbard: *Portrait of a Colonial City* (Philadelphia: Lippincott; 1939), p. 207.

28. *The New-York Gazette or the Weekly Post-Boy,* June 16, 1755. As quoted in Gottesman, *Arts and Crafts in New York,* Vol. I, p. 305.

29. As quoted in Tolles, *Meeting House and Counting House,* p. 128.

30. Alexander Hamilton: *Gentleman's Progress,* Carl Bridenbaugh, ed. (Chapel Hill: University of North Carolina Press; 1948), p. 24.

31. As quoted in Alice Morse Earle: *Two Centuries of Costume* (New York: Macmillan; 1903), Vol. II, p. 607.

32. Excerpt from a letter of Benjamin Franklin to his wife, dated London, February 19, 1758. As quoted in *The Life and Letters of Benjamin Franklin,* p. 117.

33. Excerpt from a letter of Franklin to a friend in America, dated London, March 18, 1770. As quoted, ibid. p. 176.

34. Excerpt from a letter of Franklin to the editor of a London newspaper, dated May 20, 1765. As quoted, ibid. p. 133.

35. *The Pennsylvania Gazette,* October 19, 1769, No. 2130.

36. *Autograph Collection,* MSS., The Historical Society of Pennsylvania.

37. Chambers, *Designs of Chinese Buildings,* Preface.

38. Excerpt from Franklin's letter to Mary Stevenson, dated Philadelphia, March 25, 1763. As quoted in *Life and Letters of Benjamin Franklin,* p. 131.

39. As quoted in Dagonert D. Runes and Harry G. Schrickel, eds.: *Encyclopedia of the Arts* (New York: Philosophical Library; 1946), p. 165.

40. *The New-York Gazette or the Weekly Post-Boy,* April 12, 1773. As quoted in Gottesman, *Arts and Crafts in New York,* Vol. I, p. 215.

41. Excerpt from Franklin's letter to Thomas Cushing, dated London, January 5, 1773. As quoted in *The Life and Letters of Benjamin Franklin,* p, 196.

42. John Marshall Phillips: *American Silver* (London: Max Parrish; 1949), p. 96.

43. Excerpt from Franklin's letter to Thomas Cushing, dated London, January 5, 1773. As quoted in *The Life and Letters of Benjamin Franklin,* p. 196.

44. Philip Vickers Fithian: *Journal and Letters* (Williamsburg: Colonial Williamsburg, Inc.; 1945), p. 79.

45. Broadside, Evans Record No. 12942, Library Company of Philadelphia.

46. Excerpts from letter of John Andrews of Boston to William Barrell, Philadelphia Merchant, December 18, 1773. *Proceedings,* Massachusetts Historical Society, Vol. VII, pp. 325, 326.

47. Elbridge Henry Goss: *The Life of Colonel Paul Revere* (Boston, 1891), Vol. I, p. 128, note.

48. Excerpt from a letter of Adams to his wife, dated Falmouth, July 6, 1774. As quoted in Charles Francis Adams, *Familiar Letters of John Adams and His Wife Abigail Adams* (New York: Hurd and Houghton; 1876), p. 18.

49. *Papers of the Shippen Family,* MSS., Vol. VII, The Historical Society of Pennsylvania.

50. Fithian, *Journal and Letters,* p. 147.

51. *Virginia Historical Register,* Vol. VI, p. 218.

52. As quoted in Marshall B. Davidson, *Life in America,* Vol. I, p. 134.

53. Philip Vickers Fithian: *Journal, 1775–1776* (Princeton: Princeton University Press; 1934), p. 151.

54. J. Hector St. John de Crèvecœur: *Letters from an American Farmer* (New York: Dutton; 1957), p. 39.

55. This paragraph is based on the *Journal of the Empress of China,* photostat in The Historical Society of Pennsylvania.

Bibliography

For the reader whose interest may have been aroused by this narrative, and who wishes to dig deeper for himself, the following bibliography may be of some help.

The Encyclopaedia Britannica, 14th edition, *The Oxford English Dictionary on Historical Principles,* and *The Oxford Dictionary of Quotations* are basic and full of leads.

For a glimpse of Portugal, I read *Iter Lusitanicum: or the Portugal Voyage,* by H. S. a Cosmopolite "Who though he publish this, conceals his name" (London, 1662), and *Portgual* by H. Morse Stephens (London: T. Fisher Unwin; 1908).

As for Catherine, the only documented biography I could find in English was *Catherine of Bragança* by Lillias C. Davidson (London: John Murray; 1908); however, there are sidelights on her in *Madame,* by Julia Cartwright (New York: E. P. Dutton & Co.; 1901), and in *King Charles II,* by Arthur Bryant (London: Longmans, Green & Company; 1934).

But in every English journal and memoir of the Restoration, she is at least mentioned, often maligned, and sometimes diagnosed. Heading the list of contemporaneous social reporters of the time are John Evelyn, whom we know through *The Diary of John Evelyn,* edited by William Bray (New York: Everyman's Library; 1950), 2 vols.; and Samuel Pepys with his four volume *Diary and Correspondence of·Samuel Pepys* deciphered by the Rev. J. Smith (London; 1954). In addition, there were Edward Hyde, who in three volumes wrote his biography entitled the *Life of Edward, Earl of Clarendon, Written by Himself* (Oxford: Clarendon Printing House; 1859); Gilbert Burnet with his *History of His Own Time* (London: William Smith; 1847) in two volumes; Anthony Hamilton's *Memoirs of Count Gramont* (London: Chatto and Windus; 1876); and the more statistical *Angliae Notitia, or, The Present State of England,* 15th edition by Edward Chamberlayne (London, 1684). At about the same time, Edmund Waller, whom Burnet called "the great refiner of our language," wrote *Poems, &c.* (London, 1712) about the current scene.

Intimate details of the East India Company in both England and Asia fill volumes of *A Calendar of The Court Minutes, etc., of the East India Company* compiled by Ethel B. Sainsbury (Oxford: Clarendon Press; 1909). Documented, more recent histories are *The Chronicles of the East India Company Trading to China* by Hosea Ballou Morse (Cambridge: Harvard University Press; 1926) in four volumes; *Commerce and Conquest* by C. Lestock Reid (London: C. & J. Temple; 1927); *History of the Possessions of the Honourable East India Company,* R. Montgomery Martin (London: Whittaker; 1837); and *The Nabobs in England,* James M. Holzman (New York, 1926). A first-hand account is *A Voyage to China and the East Indies* by Peter Osbeck (London, 1771).

Even though Marco Polo was probably the first to describe the East in his *Book,* which makes pleasant modern reading in *The Travels of Marco Polo,* edited by Manuel Komroff (New York: Garden City Publishing Co., 1930), Richard Hakluyt collected many a tale in *The Principall Navigations, Voiages and Discoveries of the English Nation, . . . within the Compasse of these 1500 yeeres* (London; 1589); the three volume second edition of which, printed in 1598, 1599, and 1600, and entitled *The Principal Navigations, Voyages, Traffiques & Discoveries of the English Nation, . . . within the compass of these 1600 yeeres, . . .,* is available in at least one modern reprint of twelve volumes, published in Glasgow by James MacLehose & Sons, 1903, and in New York by The Macmillan Company, 1904. In the late 1660s, John Nieuhoff signed on as "steward" to a Dutch expedition to China and described his experiences in *An Embassy from the East India Company of the United Provinces to the Grand Tartar Cham, Emperor of China,* which came out in book form with illustrations and was translated into English in 1673. And in 1696, letters from China written by the Jesuit missionary Louis Le Compte were published in Paris as *Nouveaux mémoires sur l'état présent de la Chine,* and translated the next year into English as *Memoirs and Observations . . . Made in a Late Journey Through the Empire of China.* Père J. B. du Halde's *A Description of the Empire of China* came out in London in 1738. And in 1795, excerpts from these appeared in *The World Displayed, or A Curious Collection of Voyages and Travels, selected and compiled from the Writers of all Nations* by Smart, Goldsmith, & Johnson, editors (Philadelphia, 1795). Eloise Talcott Hibbert puts it all into modern perspective in *Jesuit Adventures in China: During the Reign of K'ang Hsi* (New York: E. P. Dutton & Co.; 1941).

Back in England, Alexander Pope painted fascinating word pictures of his eighteenth century in *Moral Essays* and other writings. Daniel Defoe perceptively described the social scene in his periodical *The Review,* and in his many books, especially in *A Tour thro' the whole Island of Great Britain . . . Giving a particular and diverting account of whatever is curious and worth observation* (London; 1724), 3 vols., a modern edition of which was published in two volumes as *A Tour Through England and Wales* (New York: E. P. Dutton; 1928). Then there was also Joseph Addison, whom Macaulay called the "consummate painter of life and manners," and who alternated with Richard Steele in publishing *The Spectator,* Steele having previously written *The Tatler;* while *The World* was another periodical published in London from 1753 to 1757.

About that time, lady "Bluestockings" filled their spare time by writing and collecting letters such as *The Autobiography and Correspondence of Mary Granville, Mrs. Delany,* edited by Lady Llanover (London: Richard Bentley; 1861); *Passages from the Diaries of Mrs. Philip Lybbe Powys,* edited by Emily Climenson, 1756–1818 (London: Longmans, Green, & Co.; 1899); and *Elizabeth Montagu, The Queen of the Blue Stockings,* edited by Emily Climenson (London: John Murray; 1906). In addition, *The Verney Letters of the 18th Century from the MSS at Claydon House,* edited by Margaret Maria Lady Verney (London: Longmans, Green, & Co.; 1930), gives intimate glimpses into the lives of several generations of owners of "Claydon House," now part of The National Trust of Great Britain. Horace Walpole, of course, filled library shelves with his *Memoirs, Journals, Letters,* and *Anecdotes.*

From the viewpoint of our time, W. E. Lunt recounts England's past in *History of England* (New York: Harper & Bros.; 1946); as does J. H. Plumb in *England in the Eighteenth Century* (Harmondsworth, England: Pelican Books; 1950). B. Sprague Allen discusses her social aspects in *Tides in English Taste* (1619–1800) (Cambridge: Harvard University Press; 1937), 2 vols.; John Gloag paints a full canvas of the years 1660–1830 in *Georgian Grace* (London: Adam and Charles Black; 1956); W. S. Scott describes eighteenth-century taverns, tea gardens, and spas in *Bygone Pleasures of London* (London: Marsland Publications; 1948); John Ashton compiled from original sources *Social Life in the Reign of Queen Anne* (London: Chatto & Windus; 1893); E. F. Carritt chronologically arranged contemporaneous items of artistic or social interest in *A Calendar of British Taste, 1600–1800* (London: Routledge & Kegan Paul; 1948); and Millia Davenport gathered a vast amount of fashion-oriented information into *The Book of Costume* (New York: Crown; 1948).

As for particular categories, cotton is covered admirably by M. D. C. Crawford in *The Heritage of Cotton* (New York: Grosset & Dunlap; 1924). Specifically Indian textiles are discussed by G. P. Baker in *Calico Painting and Printing in the East Indies in the XVIIth and XVIIIth Centuries* (London: Edward Arnold; 1921), and by John Irwin in *Journal of Indian Textile* (Ahmedabad, India), Vols. I and II, as well as in the *Burlington Magazine* (April 1955). On embroideries, there is A. F. Kendrick's definitive *English Needlework* (London: A. & C. Black, Ltd.; 1933).

Cane, and the Portuguese influence on furniture, is discussed by Eberlein and Ramsdell in *The Practical Book of Italian, Spanish, and Portuguese Furniture* (Philadelphia: J. B. Lippincott, Co.; 1927); by R. W. Symonds in *The Connoisseur* (April and June 1951); by Helen Comstock in *Antiques* (January 1957); and by Walter A. Dyer in *The Antiquarian* (August 1930).

As for Chinese furniture, that is authoritatively described by George N. Kates in *Chinese Household Furniture* (New York: Dover Publications; 1948); and Chinese eighteenth-century influence on English furniture can be appreciated by studying Thomas Chippendale's *The Gentleman and Cabinet-Maker's DIRECTOR: being a large COLLECTION of the most Elegant and Useful Designs of Household Furniture in the Gothic, Chinese, and Modern Taste,* . . . (London, 1754, also 1755), and to a lesser degree his revised 1762 edition, or its more available reprint (New York: Towse Publishing Co.; 1938). William Chambers's *Designs of Chinese Buildings, Furniture, Dresses, Machines and Utensils* is also a valuable document.

Lacquer-ware is a joy to read about in the contemporary *Treatise of Japanning and Varnishing* written and published by John Stalker in 1688. More recent texts consulted were Esther Singleton's *Dutch and Flemish Furniture* (New York: McClure; 1902); Margaret Jourdain and R. Soame Jenyns's *Chinese Export Art* (London: Country Life Ltd.; 1950); and Joseph Downs's *American Furniture* (New York: The Macmillan Company; 1952).

Tea, from the eighteenth-century point of view, is discussed by John Cookley Lettsom in *The Natural History of the Tea-Tree* (London, 1772). Its economic and social history is followed by Gervas Huxley in *Talking of Tea* (London: Thames and Hudson; 1956); in Agnes Repplier's *To Think of Tea!* (Boston: Houghton Mifflin; 1932); and in Yasunosuke Fukukita's *Tea Cult of Japan* (Tokyo: Japan Travel Bureau; 1955). Its accouterments are described in *English Domestic Silver* by Charles Oman (London: Adam

& Charles Black; 1949); in *Old Silver in Modern Settings,* Edward Wenham (New York: Alfred A. Knopf; 1951); and in *Three Centuries of English Domestic Silver,* Bernard and Therle Hughes (New York: Wilfred Funk, Inc.; 1952). Definitive articles relating to tea were written by G. Bernard Hughes in *Country Life* (September 8, 1955); and by Judith Burling and Mabel Irene Huggins in *Antiques* (April 1942).

To understand the eighteenth-century feeling for porcelain, read "Old China" by Charles Lamb in his *Essays of Elia*. There is also the learned *History of the Ceramic Art* by Albert Jacquemart (New York: Scribner, Armstrong & Co.; 1877), which was written while the old legends were still remembered and scientific analysis was unheard of. More recent works are W. B. Honey's *English Pottery and Porcelain* (London: A. & C. Black, Ltd.; 1933); George Savage's *Porcelain Through the Ages* (Harmondsworth, England: Pelican Books; 1954); John Spargo's *Early American Pottery and China* (New York: The Century Co.; 1926); Eliza Meteyard's two volume *Life and Works of Wedgwood* (London: Hurst and Blackett; 1865); John Goldsmith Phillips's *China-Trade Porcelain* (Cambridge: Harvard University Press; 1956); and J. A. Lloyd Hyde and Ricardo R. Espirito's *Chinese Porcelain for the European Market* (Lisbon: Editions R. E. S. M.; 1956).

As for "Chinese Taste" in practically everything, that has been ably covered in *A Cycle of Cathay,* William W. Appleton (New York: Columbia University Press; 1951). As it applies particularly to furniture, read *English Furniture, The Georgian Period* by Margaret Jourdain and F. Rose (London: B. T. Batsford Ltd.; 1953); and for a commercial fairy tale, *The Story of the Willow Plate* by Jane Campbell (Philadelphia; n.d.). Otherwise, nearly every book previously mentioned is in some way concerned with the Chinese Taste.

Even in America, busy men wrote journals, diaries, and letters. Those consulted for the last chapter were *The Life and Letters of Benjamin Franklin* (Eau Claire, Wisconsin: E. M. Hale & Company; n.d.); Samuel Sewall's *Diary, 1674–1729* (Collections of the Massachusetts Historical Society, 5th series, 1878) and his *Letter Book, 1686–1729* (Collections of the Massachusetts Historical Society, 6th series, 1886 and 1888); Dr. Alexander Hamilton's *Gentleman's Progress,* edited by Carl Bridenbaugh (Chapel Hill: University of North Carolina Press; 1948); *Familiar Letters of John Adams and his Wife Abigail Adams,* edited by Charles Francis Adams (New York: Hurd and Houghton; 1876); Philip Vickers Fithian's *Journal and Letters* (Williamsburg: Colonial Williamsburg, Inc.: 1945) and *Journal, 1775–1776* (Princeton: Princeton University Press; 1934); *Letters from an American Farmer,*

J. Hector St. John de Crévecoeur (New York: E. P. Dutton & Co., Inc.; 1957); and twelve volumes of *The Writings of George Washington,* Jared Sparks (Boston: Ferdinand Andrews; 1839).

As for contemporary American histories, *The History and Present State of Virginia* [1705] by Robert Beverley (Chapel Hill: University of North Carolina Press; 1947); *The History of New England* by Daniel Neal (London, 1720); and *The Present State of Virginia* [1724] by Hugh Jones (Chapel Hill: University of North Carolina Press; 1956) give the flavor of the times.

Present-day histories bring all the colonies into focus: *The First Americans,* Thomas Jefferson Wertenbaker (New York: The Macmillan Company; 1929); *The Growth of the American Republic,* Samuel E. Morison and Henry S. Commager (New York: Oxford University Press; 1951); *The American Heritage Book of the Revolution* (New York: American Heritage; 1958); and *Life in America,* 2 vols., Marshall B. Davidson (Boston: Houghton Mifflin Co.; 1951).

Definitive books of more limited scope include *Cities in Revolt,* Carl Bridenbaugh (New York: Alfred A. Knopf, Inc.; 1955); *Meeting House and Counting House,* Frederick B. Tolles (Chapel Hill: University of North Carolina Press; 1948); *Portrait of a Colonial City,* Harold D. Eberlein and Courtlandt V. Hubbard (Philadelphia: J. B. Lippincott Co.; 1939); *The Spirit of 'Seventy-Six,* 2 vols., Henry S. Commager and Richard B. Morris, editors (New York: The Bobbs-Merrill Co.; 1958); *History of the City of New York,* John W. Leonard (New York: Joseph and Sefton; 1910); *Dutch New York,* Esther Singleton (New York: Dodd, Mead & Co.; 1909); and *Elihu Yale,* Hiram Bingham (New York: Dodd, Mead & Co.; 1939).

Books of specific interest included *The Furniture of Our Forefathers,* 2 vols., by Esther Singleton (New York: Doubleday, Page & Co.; 1900); *American Silver,* John Marshall Phillips (London: Max Parrish & Co.; 1949); and *Two Centuries of Costume,* 2 vols., Alice Morse Earle (New York: The Macmillan Company; 1903).

The manuscripts examined were David Garrick's draft letter in the *Theatre Collection* of the Harvard College Library, the Powell letter in the *Autograph Collection* of The Historical Society of Pennsylvania, the *Papers of the Shippen Family,* and the *Journal* of the *Empress of China,* also in The Historical Society of Pennsylvania.

When it comes to newspapers, reading the advertisements listed in *The Arts and Crafts in Philadelphia,* A. C. Prime (Topsfield, Mass.: Walpole Society; 1929); *The Arts and Crafts in New England,* George F. Dow (Topsfield, Mass.: The Wayside Press; 1927); and *The Arts and Crafts of New York*, Rita S. Gottesman (New York: New-York Historical Society; 1938) is only slightly less exciting than perusing the actual newspapers, such as *The Pennsylvania Gazette* and *The Pennsylvania Chronicle*, which were read for *Richer than Spices.*

Index

A NOTE ON THE TYPE

THE TEXT of this book has been set on the Linotype in a typeface called *Baskerville*. The face is a facsimile reproduction of types cast from molds made for John Baskerville (1706–1775) from his designs. The punches for the revived Linotype Baskerville were cut under the supervision of the English printer George W. Jones. John Baskerville's original face was one of the forerunners of the type-style known as "modern face" to printers: a "modern" of the period 1800.

This book was composed and bound by
The Haddon Craftsmen, Inc., Scranton, Pa.
Printed by Halliday Lithograph Corp., West Hanover, Mass.
Typography and binding design by Albert Burkhardt